ESSENTIAL NAPLAN

NUMERACY

NAPLAN*-Format Practice Tests with Worked Solutions

*These tests have been produced by Five Senses Education Pty Ltd independently of Australian governments and are not officially endorsed publications of the NAPLAN program

RAY LEE | JIMMY LIU

To Cookie, my light,
and to Phoebe who I hope
can one day figure out all the questions in this book.

Five Senses Education Pty Ltd
2/195 Prospect Highway
Seven Hills 2147
New South Wales Australia

First Published 2023

Lee, Ray and Liu, Jimmy

Essential NAPLAN*
Numeracy Year 2
NAPLAN*-Format Practice Tests with Worked Solutions

ISBN 978-1-76032-548-0

* These tests have been produced by Five Senses Education Pty Ltd
independently of Australian governments and are not officially
endorsed publications of the NAPLAN program

2025 01 03

Contents

Preface

This book is designed to help students prepare for the NAPLAN Test. It consists of seven numeracy practice exam papers and is suitable for use by Year 2 students. The exam papers are designed to the exact format of the NAPLAN Numeracy Test, with hand-picked questions that closely relate to past NAPLAN Examination questions.

Success in this competitive exam requires commitment and hard work. We hope these practice exam papers can help you achieve your goals.

Five Senses Education

Year 2 NAPLAN*-Format

NUMERACY PRACTICE TEST 1

Instructions

- There are 35 questions.
- You have 45 minutes to complete the test.
- You have to shade one bubble for each multiple-choice question.
- Write your answer in the box for short answer questions.

NAME : ______________________ **SCORE :__________**

1 A merry-go-round turns three times each minute.

How many times does it turn in 5 minutes?

5	10	15	20
☐	☐	☐	☐

2 Which of these shapes is a triangular prism?

☐ ☐ ☐ ☐

3 32 marbles are shared equally between 4 people.

How many marbles does each person get?

☐

4 What time is shown on this clock?

6:30 ☐ 7:00 ☐ 7:30 ☐ 8:30 ☐

5 Look at these numbers:

105 210 305 390

Find the pair of numbers which have a difference of 95.

105 and 210 ☐ 210 and 305 ☐ 305 and 390 ☐ 210 and 390 ☐

6 Vivian buys a skirt for $27 and some shoes for $15.

How much does she spend altogether?

$12 ☐ $27 ☐ $32 ☐ $42 ☐

7 Jayden starts a sequence with the number 14.

He uses the rule 'add 8' to make the sequence.

What is the 4th number in the sequence?

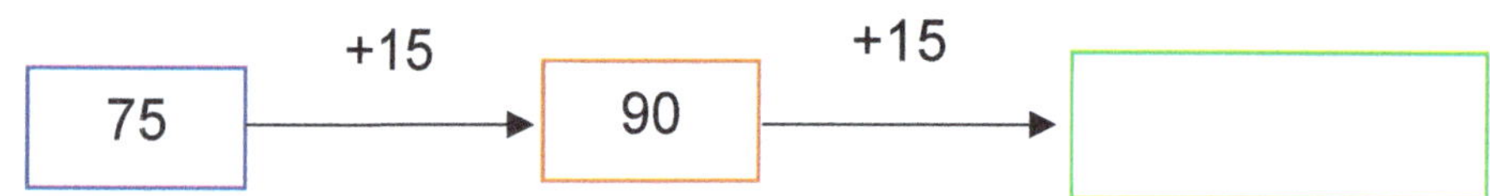

32 ☐ 38 ☐ 40 ☐ 42 ☐

8 What is the next number in this pattern?

75 —+15→ 90 —+15→ ☐

9 The table below shows how many children in Year 2 brought each type of fruit to school.

Fruit	Number of children
Apple	7
Banana	3
Orange	1
Pear	2
Peach	4

How many apples, bananas and pears were there in total?

☐

10 Alan's puppies weigh 5 kg, 13 kg and 8 kg.
How much do they weigh altogether?

11 What is the next number in this pattern?

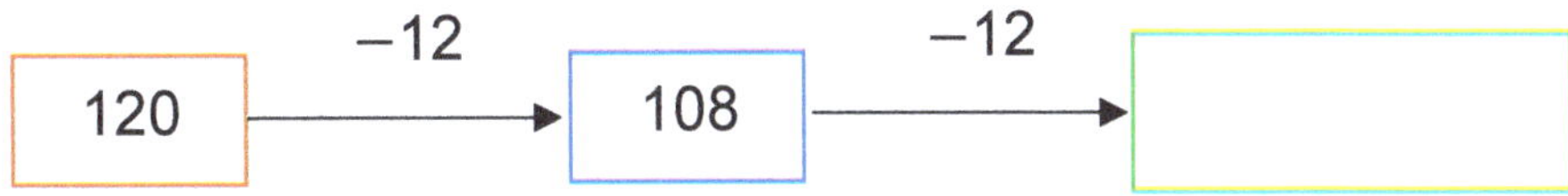

12 Jasmin asked some people whether they liked strawberry, chocolate or vanilla ice cream.

Her results are shown in the bar chart below.

How many people did Jasmin ask altogether?

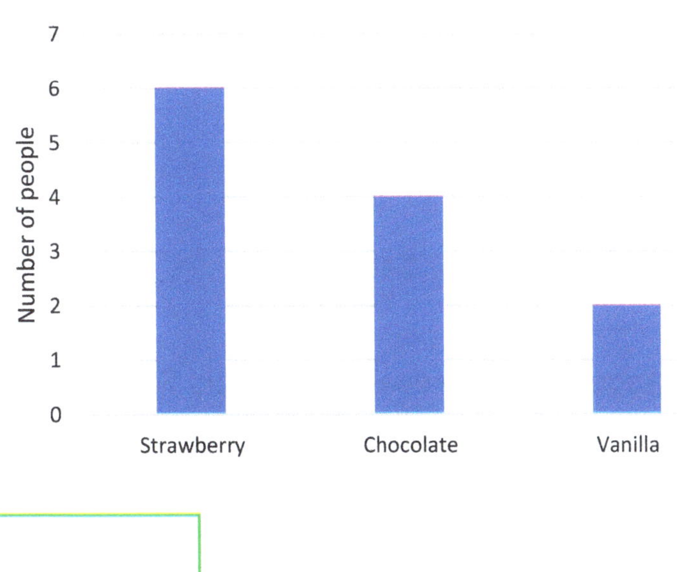

13 How many lines of symmetry does this shape have?

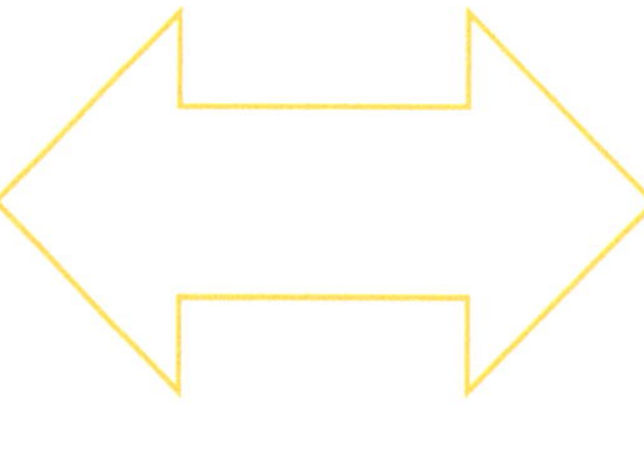

14 Mark has 9 rabbits. Each rabbit eats 6 carrots a day.

How many carrots do they eat in total each day?

9 ☐ 18 ☐ 27 ☐ 54 ☐

15 Jack bought 2 bottles of apple juice and 2 cartons of milk.
The picture below shows how much each item cost.

$3.00

$4.50

How much change will Jack receive if he paid $20.00?

16 This is a solid 3D object.

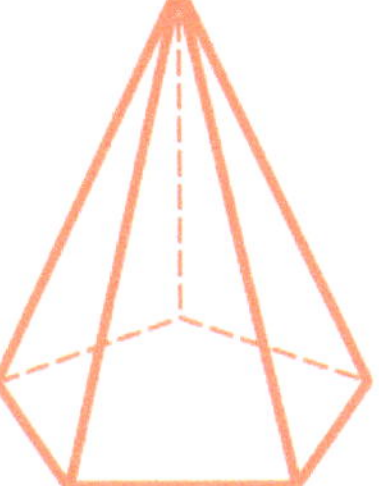

How many faces does the object have?

5	6	7	10
☐	☐	☐	☐

17 Tom has $8. He needs $3.50 more to buy a comic book.

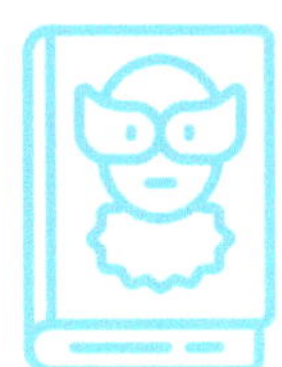

How much is the comic book? ☐

18 Which clock below shows a quarter past ten?

☐ ☐ ☐ ☐

19 My sister is 128 cm tall. I am 12 cm taller and my big brother is 5 cm taller than me. How tall is he?

135 cm ☐ 140 cm ☐ 145 cm ☐ 150 cm ☐

20 Olivia is packing 18 cakes into boxes.
Each full box holds 4 cakes.

What is the smallest number of boxes Olivia needs to pack all the cakes?

☐

21 Multiply me by 2 and then divide the answer by 3 and you will get 4.
What am I?

☐ 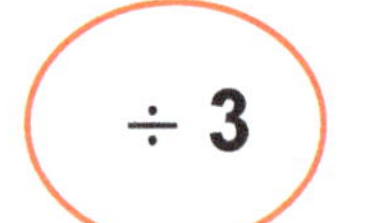

= **4**

6 ☐ 7 ☐ 8 ☐ 9 ☐

22 Choose the shape that is the correct reflection of the following shape.

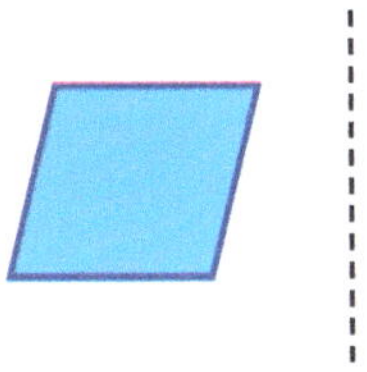

?

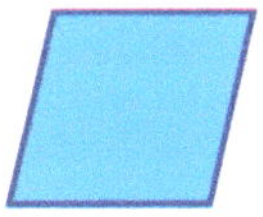

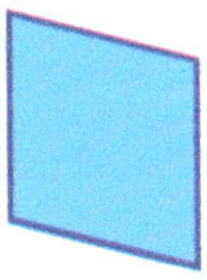

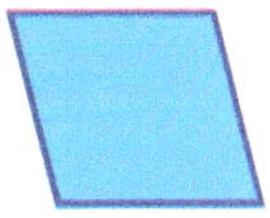

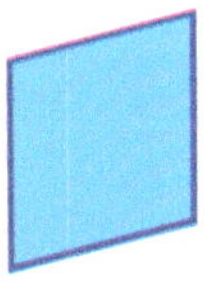

23 The table below shows the timetable for a school bus.

Departure time	Arrival time
8:00 am	8:15 am
8:30 am	8:45 am
9:00 am	9:15 am

How long does it take to get to school by bus?

minutes

24 Emma takes an object from each of the following boxes without looking.

Which box gives Emma the best chance of taking a  ?

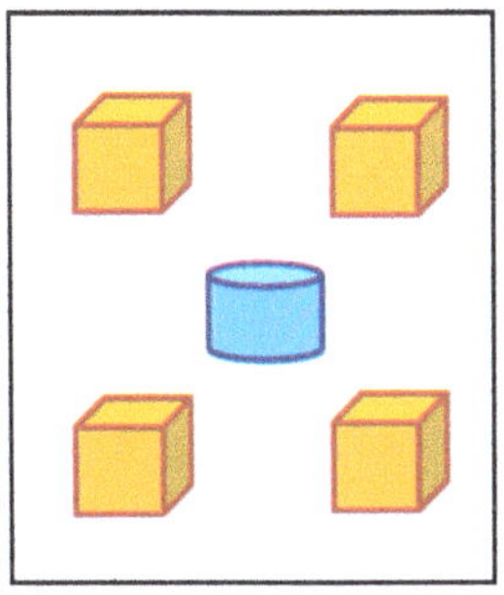

25 Sophia wants to buy some umbrellas. Each umbrella costs $8.

How many can she buy with $48?

4 ☐ 5 ☐ 6 ☐ 7 ☐

26 Which figure comes next in the following sequence?

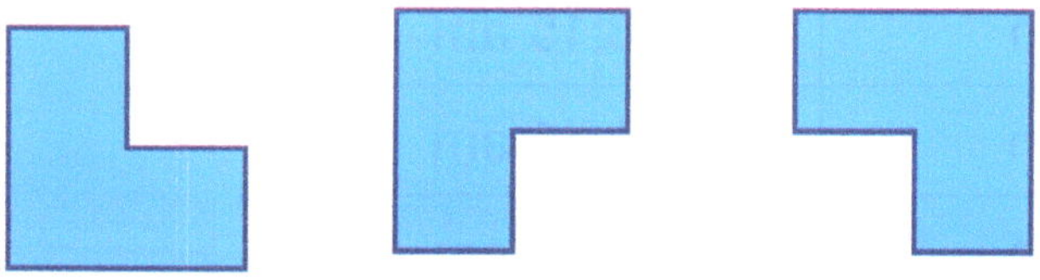

?

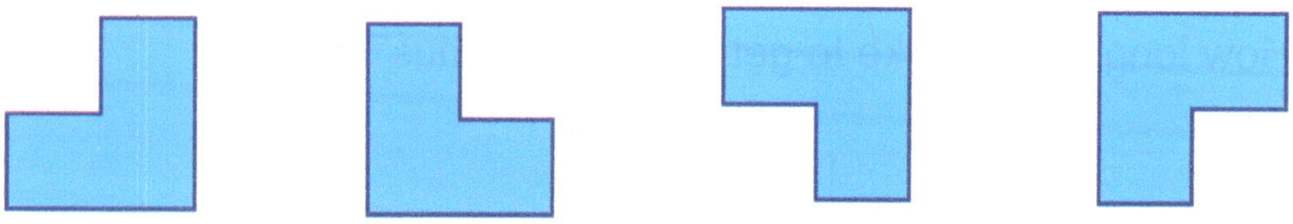

☐ ☐ ☐ ☐

27 A bucket holds 9 litres. 4 buckets of water fill a tank.
How many litres of water does the tank hold?

28 Harry had 75 tomatoes in his shed. 3 of them were rotten.
He packed the rest into packs of 9 to sell on the side of the road.

How many packets of tomatoes did he get?

☐

29 What is the next number in this pattern?

7, 11, 15, 19, ☐

30 The bell to go into school is at 9:00. The next bell for recess is two hours after that.

What time does recess begin?

10:00 ☐ 11:00 ☐ 12:00 ☐ 12:30 ☐

31 In my money box I found I had these coins:

2 fifty-cent coins

3 twenty-cent coins

5 ten-cent coins

How much money do I have altogether?

$1.90 ☐ $2.00 ☐ $2.10 ☐ $2.20 ☐

32 An apple costs half as much as a peach.

If a peach costs $1.60, how much would 5 apples cost?

$1.60

$3.00 ☐ $3.60 ☐ $3.80 ☐ $4.00 ☐

33 Which one of the following scissors is opened at the widest angle?

☐ ☐ ☐ ☐

34 If two jars fit into this space.

How many jars will fit into this space?

8	16	24	32
☐	☐	☐	☐

35 Today is Wednesday and Mia's birthday is next Tuesday.
How many days are there until her birthday?

☐

Year 2 NAPLAN*-Format
NUMERACY PRACTICE TEST 2

Instructions

- There are 35 questions.
- You have 45 minutes to complete the test.
- You have to shade one bubble for each multiple-choice question.
- Write your answer in the box for short answer questions.

NAME : ______________________ **SCORE :**__________

NUMERACY YEAR 2

1 What is the **perimeter** of this shape?

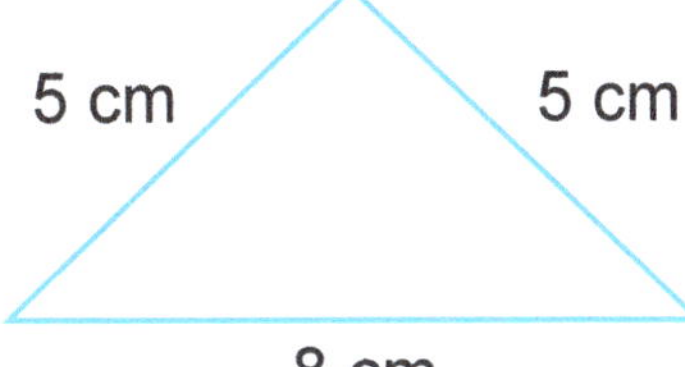

- [ ] 18 cm
- [ ] 25 cm
- [ ] 36 cm
- [ ] 40 cm

2 There are 176 men and 105 women at a sports club.

How many people are there altogether?

3 What is the total value of these coins?

4 The table below shows the number of blue, yellow and red cars that passed our house on Sunday.

Blue cars	Yellow cars	Red cars
37	29	14

How many cars passed the house altogether?

60 ☐ 70 ☐ 80 ☐ 90 ☐

5 There are 104 pages in a book and Olivia has read 55 pages.

How many more pages does she have to read to finish the book?

41 ☐ 49 ☐ 51 ☐ 59 ☐

6 Jonathan was counting by tens. He began at 15.

What are the numbers ten before and ten after 95?

 95 

85, 105 ☐ 90, 100 ☐ 94, 96 ☐ 80, 100 ☐

7 What was the step to change the position of the shape below on the left to the shape on the right?

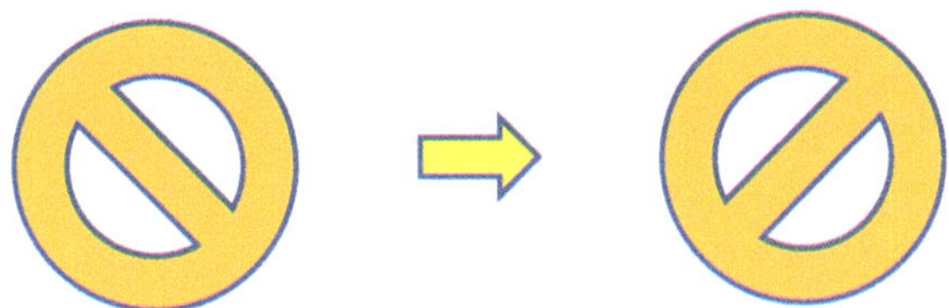

slide ☐ turn by 90° ☐ turn by 180° ☐ turn by 360° ☐

8 What is the next number in this pattern?

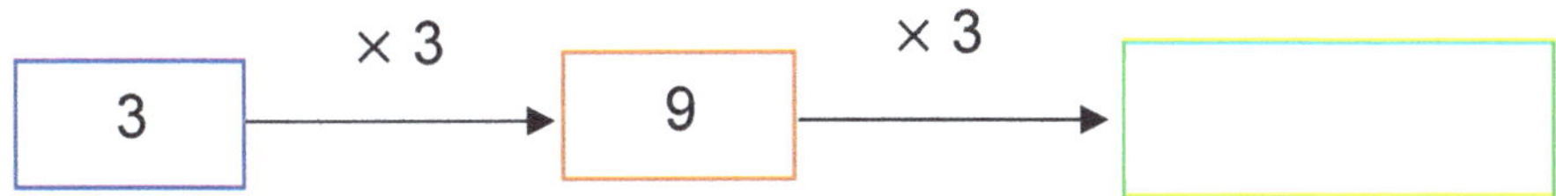

9 Mia had $20. She bought a pencil for $2.50 and a pencil case $4.50.

How much did she have left?

$2.50 **$4.50**

10 A note-book costs $2.50. A dictionary costs 3 times as much.

How much do I pay for 1 note book and 1 dictionary?

$2.50

$4.50 ☐ $5.00 ☐ $7.50 ☐ $10.00 ☐

11 There were 24 cherries to share among 6 people.

How many could they have each?

☐

12 My change from $5.00 was 2 fifty-cent coins and two ten-cent coins.

How much did I spend?

☐

13 The length of a rope is 3 metres. It is cut into 6 equal pieces. How long is each piece?

☐ cm

14 Which of the numbers below is the closest to 100?

90	95	102	110
☐	☐	☐	☐

15 Peter just missed the 10:45 ferry to the zoo.

The next ferry leaves in 20 minutes.

What time will that be on the clock?

☐ ☐ ☐ ☐

16 How many pictures is $\frac{1}{2}$ of 10 pictures?

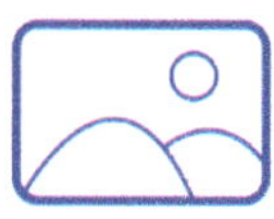 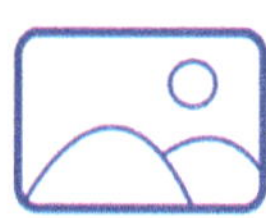 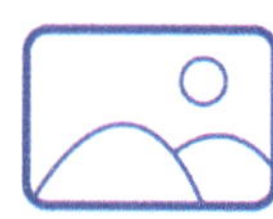 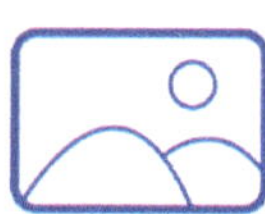 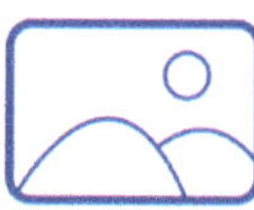

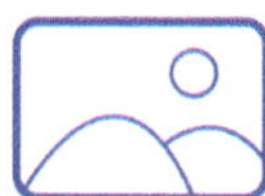 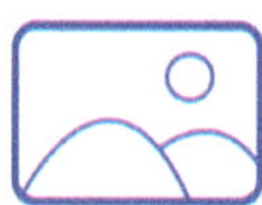   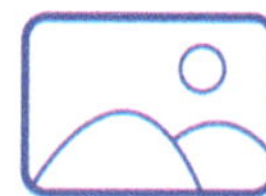

2 ☐ 3 ☐ 5 ☐ 10 ☐

17 What is the difference between the biggest and the smallest number in the following set?

165 97 201 79 102

96 ☐ 99 ☐ 104 ☐ 122 ☐

18 This is half the money I found in my money box.

What is the total amount of money in my money box?

☐

19 Farmer James had 12 cows. A quarter of these cows were brown and the rest were black and white.

How many black and white cows did he have?

☐

20 How many cubes have been used to build the 3D shape below?

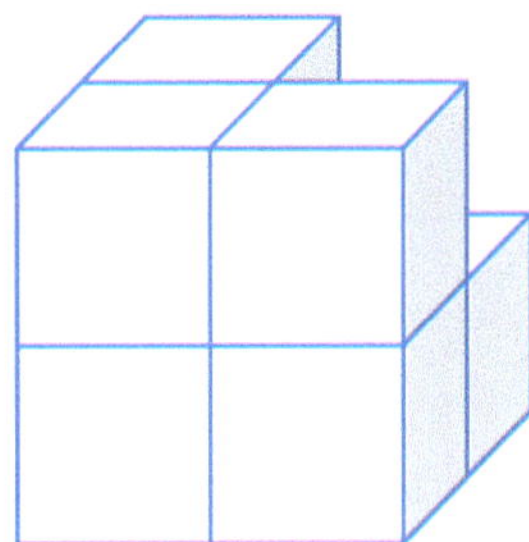

4 ☐ 5 ☐ 6 ☐ 7 ☐

21 How many whole squares are shaded in this figure?

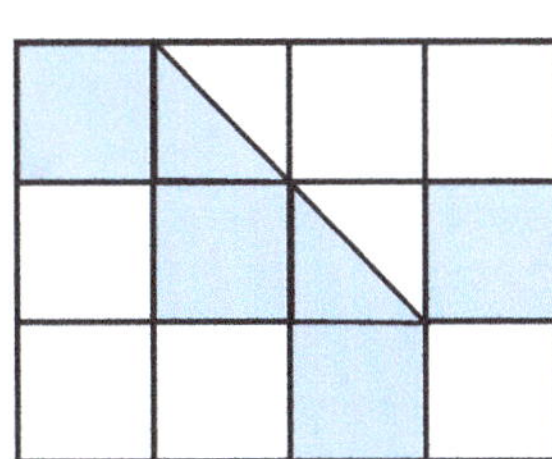

4 ☐ 5 ☐ 6 ☐ 7 ☐

22

Menu Items	Price
Raisin Toast	$7.00
Bacon & Egg Roll	$9.00
Orange Juice	$4.50

If I order one raisin toast and one orange juice, how much do I have to pay?

23 Which fraction of this pizza has been cut away?

24 Which shape comes next?

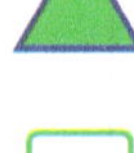

NUMERACY YEAR 2

25

83 – 38 = ? + 16

What is the missing value?

23	29	34	45
☐	☐	☐	☐

26 Which clock correctly shows 3:45?

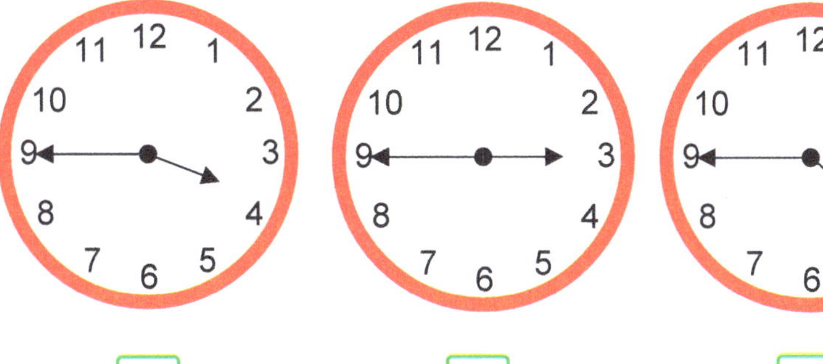
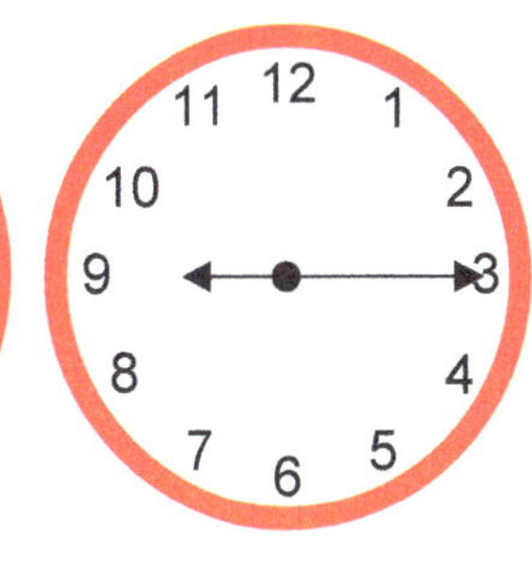

☐ ☐ ☐ ☐

27 Choose the option that is **not** a rotation of the following image.

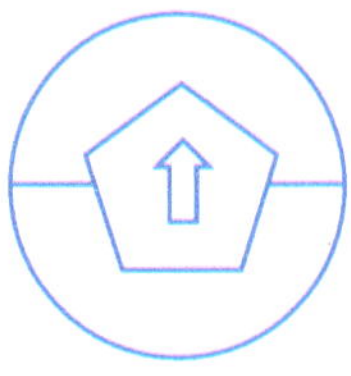

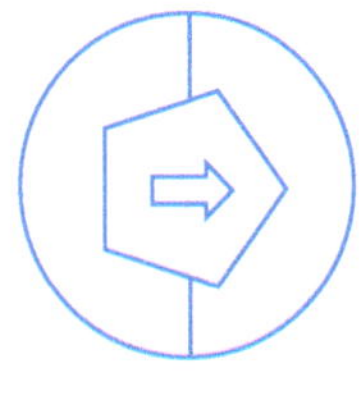

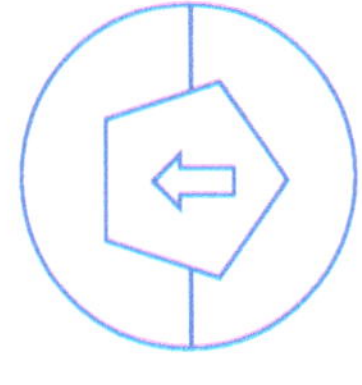
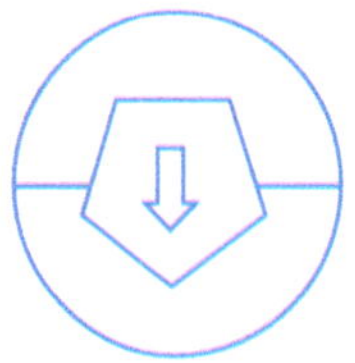

☐ ☐ ☐ ☐

28 The graph below shows the different ways children from Sydney Primary School get to school.

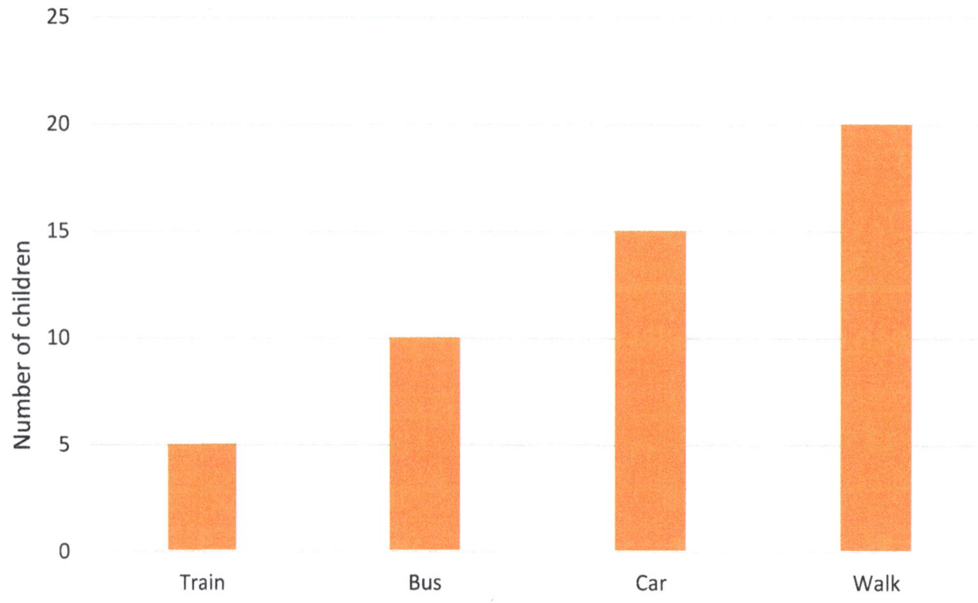

How many children went to school by car?

29 What is the next number in the following pattern?

3, 8, 13, 18,

30 Mr William splits his class into teams of four for a quiz.
There are 32 children in the class.

How many teams will there be?

6 ☐ 7 ☐ 8 ☐ 9 ☐

31 This set of steps needs to be one row higher.

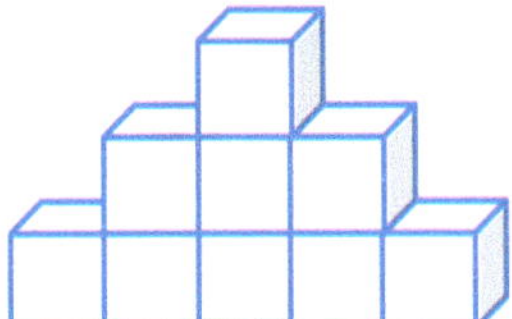

How many more blocks are needed?

6	7	8	9
☐	☐	☐	☐

32 Which of the following instructions lead from home to the library?

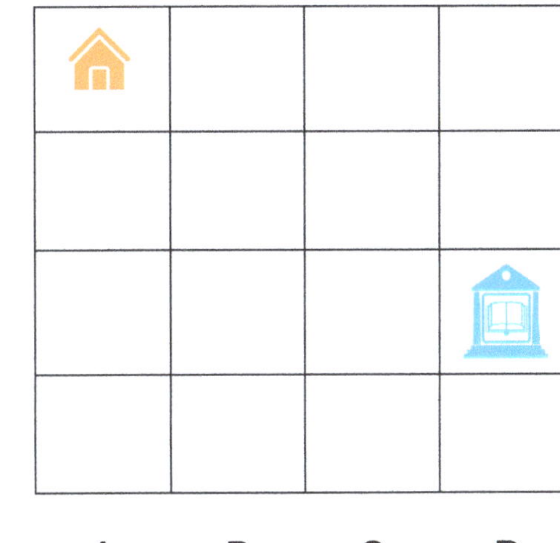

☐ South 1 square, east 3 squares

☐ South 2 squares, east 3 squares

☐ South 2 squares, west 3 squares

☐ South 3 squares, west 2 squares

33 Form the **largest** 3-digit number with the digits below.

2  3 

34 What value should the ☐ be to make the following algorithm true?

$$\begin{array}{r} 2\ 5\ 0 \\ -\quad \square\ 8 \\ \hline 1\ 9\ 2 \end{array}$$

5 ☐ 6 ☐ 8 ☐ 9 ☐

35 The following books are on display in a bookshelf.

If the blue book and the red book swap places, which book is 2nd in line from the right?

Year 2 NAPLAN*-Format

NUMERACY PRACTICE TEST 3

Instructions

- There are 35 questions.
- You have 45 minutes to complete the test.
- You have to shade one bubble for each multiple-choice question.
- Write your answer in the box for short answer questions.

NAME : ______________________ **SCORE :**__________

1 5 hundreds, 3 tens and 14 ones is the same as ____________.

Hundreds	Tens	Ones
● ● ● ● ●	● ● ●	● ● ● ● ● ● ● ● ● ● ● ● ● ●

534 ☐ 537 ☐ 544 ☐ 634 ☐

2 What number fills in the blank below?

$$25 \times 4 = 23 \times 5 - \square$$

12 ☐ 13 ☐ 15 ☐ 16 ☐

3 The table below shows each student's favourite subject.

Name	Favourite subject
Renee	English
James	English
Kevin	Maths
Cindy	Maths
Amy	English

How many students have English as their favourite subject?

☐ students

NUMERACY YEAR 2

4 Liam went shopping and bought 3 t-shirts costing $30 each and 2 jackets costing $70 each.
How much did he spend?

$30.00 **$70.00**

$150 ☐ $230 ☐ $270 ☐ $290 ☐

5 If John had to pay $10 for his smartphone every month for 2 years, how much does he have to pay in total?

$20 ☐ $120 ☐ $240 ☐ $480 ☐

6 Choose the correct number that fits the following rule.

1	2	3	8	9	10	15	?	17	22

14 ☐ 16 ☐ 18 ☐ 20 ☐

7 Starting at 6, the number is multiplied by 2.
Which of the following is part of the rule?

18 ☐ 22 ☐ 36 ☐ 48 ☐

8 What is the next number in this pattern?

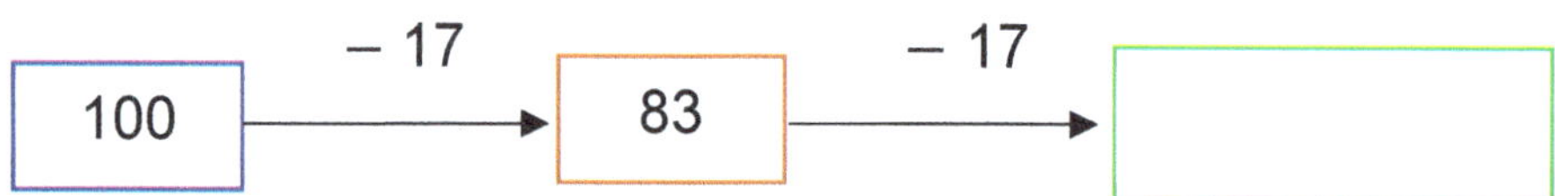

9 Andy asked Year 2 children what their favourite sport was.
The results are tallied below.

Tennis	||
Soccer	卌 卌 卌
Cricket	卌 ||||
Golf	|

How many children did Andy survey?

27 ☐ 30 ☐ 33 ☐ 35 ☐

10 How many edges does the following object have?

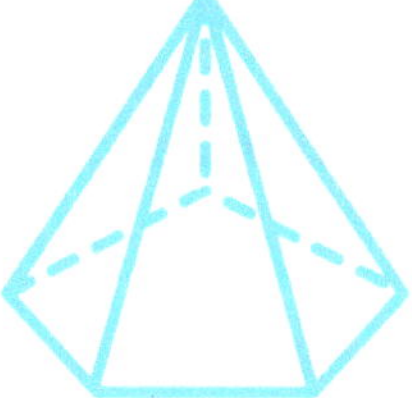

11 What is the next number in this pattern?

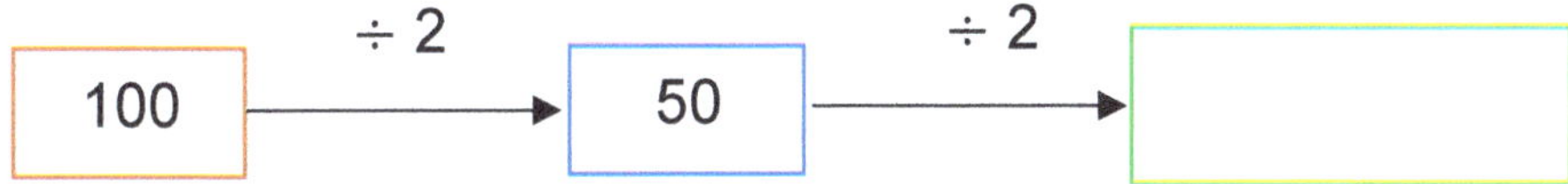

12 Nicolas has 5 twenty-cent coins and 5 ten-cent coins.

How much money does he have altogether?

$1.50 ☐ $1.70 ☐ $1.90 ☐ $2.00 ☐

13 What number is the arrow pointing to on the number line below?

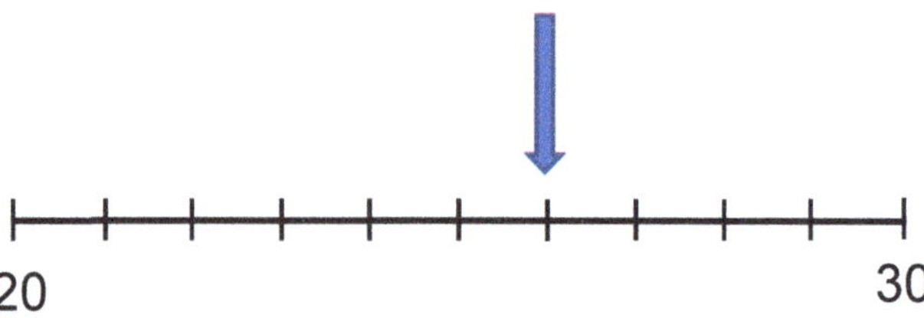

21 ☐ 26 ☐ 27 ☐ 34 ☐

14 The total length of rope A and rope B is 390 cm.

The length of rope A is 140 cm.

What is the length of rope B?

220 cm ☐ 230 cm ☐ 240 cm ☐ 250 cm ☐

15 Charlie shoots three paintballs at a target as below.

His total score is found by adding up the points for each paintball.

What is his total score?

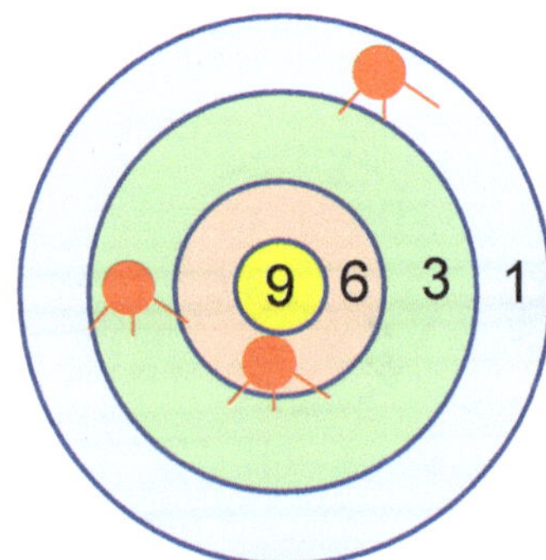

☐

16 Which of the shapes below has exactly two right angles?

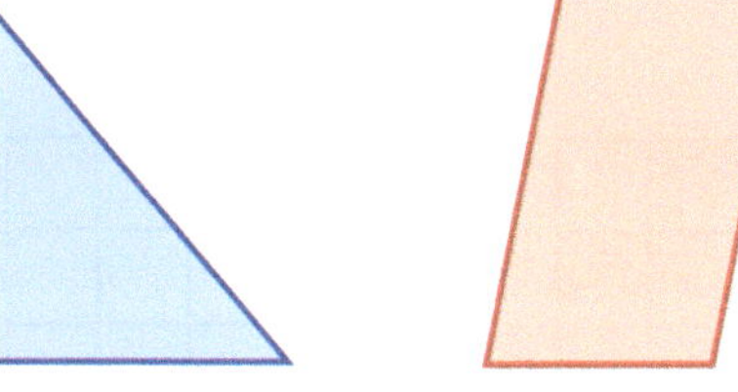

17 Patricia's clock is shown on the right. It is 15 minutes ahead of the correct time.

What is the correct time?

18 What fraction of this square shaded?

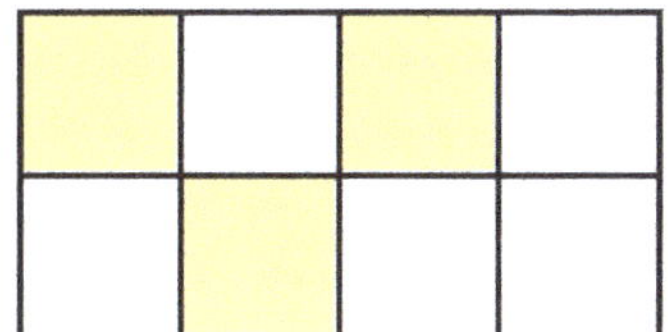

$\frac{1}{3}$ $\frac{3}{5}$ $\frac{3}{8}$ $\frac{5}{8}$

19 The shaded figures below are made up of 1 cm squares.

Which figure has the largest shaded area?

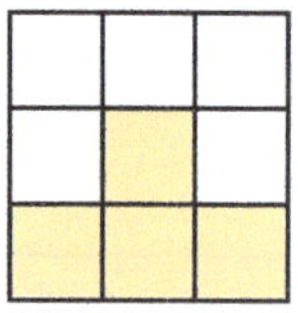

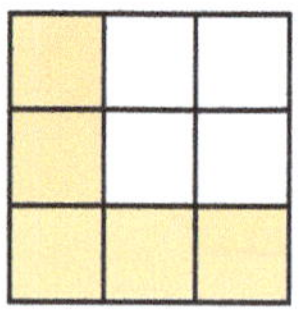

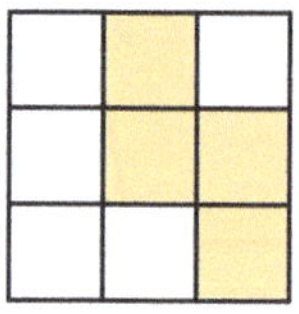

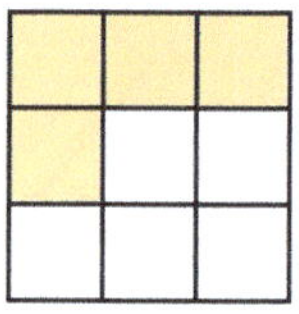

☐ ☐ ☐ ☐

20 Which of the following statements is true?

☐ A pentagon has 4 sides.

☐ A triangle has 2 angles.

☐ A rectangle has curved sides.

☐ A hexagon has 6 sides.

21 What is the front view of this object?

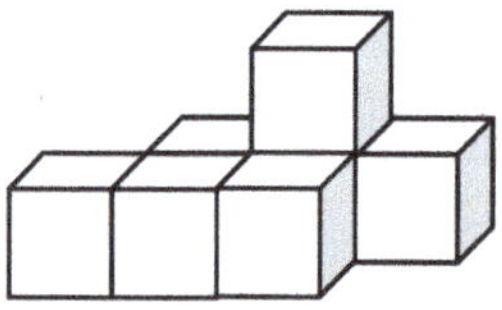

Front

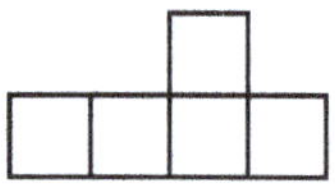

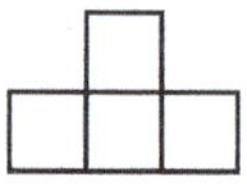

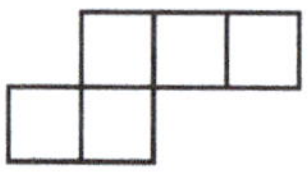

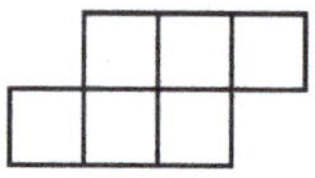

☐ ☐ ☐ ☐

22 What is the biggest number you can make using these four digits? You can only use each card once.

9 4 2 7

23 Some squares on the grid below are shaded.

What is the smallest number of extra squares that must be shaded to make this pattern symmetrical?

24 What shape is the party hat below?

cube ☐ cylinder ☐ sphere ☐ cone ☐

25 A bag of flour weighs 7 kg while a bag of rice weighs 3 kg.
If a bag of rocks weighs 9 kg more than the bag of rice, how much heavier is the bag of rocks than the bag of flour?

Flour (7 kg)

Rice (3 kg)

3 kg	4 kg	5 kg	7 kg
☐	☐	☐	☐

26 Glue sticks at the stationery store cost $1.50 each. Sean had $6.00.

How many glue sticks could he buy?

2	3	4	5
☐	☐	☐	☐

27 In a playground, there are benches which can sit 6 children each.
If there are 12 benches, how many children can sit down?

☐

28 What is the largest shaded fraction of these images?

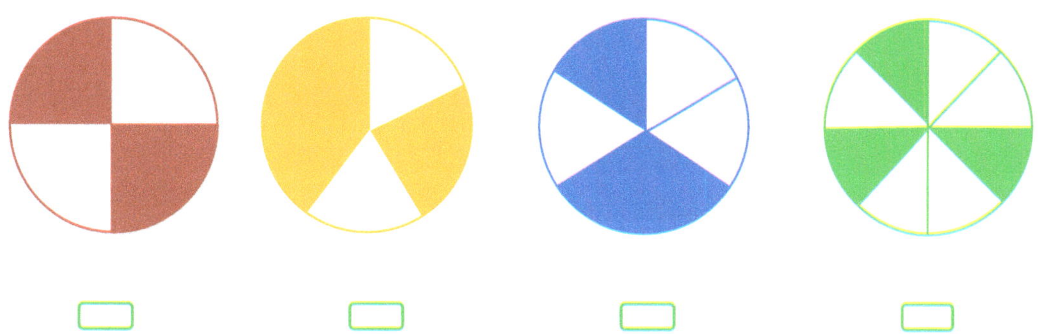

☐ ☐ ☐ ☐

29 What is the missing number in the pattern?

2, 8, ☐ , 20, 26

30

November						
SUN	MON	TUE	WED	THU	FRI	SAT
		1	2	3	4	5
6	7	8	9	10	11	12
13	14	15	16	17	18	19
20	21	22	23	24	25	26
27	28	29	30			

What is the first day of December?

Sunday ☐ Monday ☐ Thursday ☐ Wednesday ☐

31 Which one of the triangles below is isosceles?

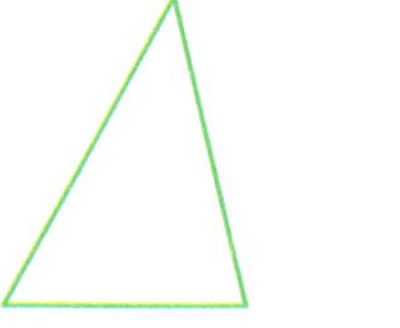 ☐

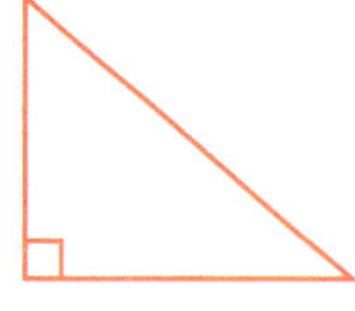 ☐

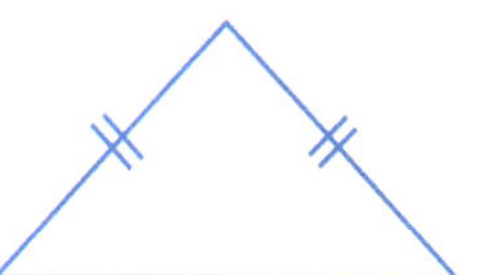 ☐

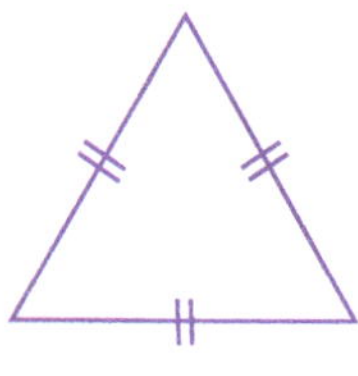 ☐

32 Jonathan looked at the colour of the cars in a car park.
He made a pictogram of his results below.

Red	🚗 🚗 🚗
Blue	🚗 🚗
Green	🚗
Grey	🚗 🚗 🚗 🚗

Each 🚗 = 4 cars

How many blue cars were there?

☐ cars

33 I got to the bus stop at 8:40 am, but missed the bus by 10 minutes.

Buses arrive every $\frac{1}{2}$ hour. What time will the next bus come?

08:50	09:00	09:10	09:20
☐	☐	☐	☐

34 Alex had $25.00. His father gave him $30.00.
How much more will he need to buy a scooter worth $80.00?

$80.00

☐

35 Which of the shapes below have 8 corners?

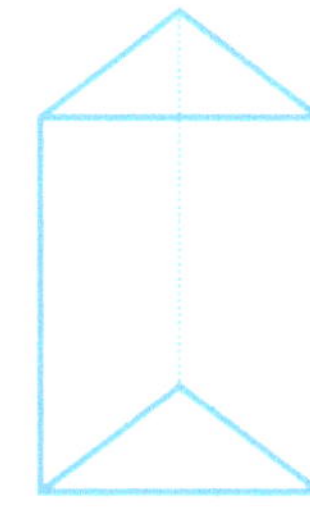

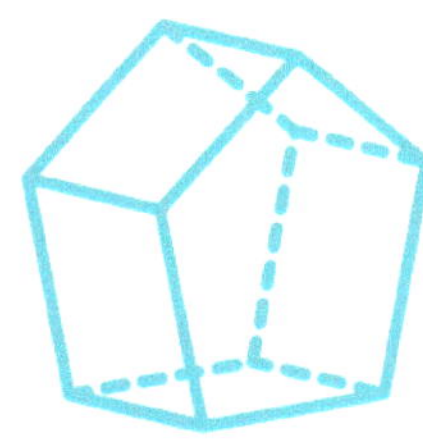

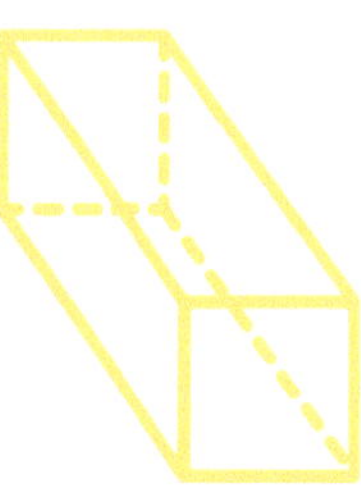

☐ ☐ ☐ ☐

Year 2 NAPLAN*-Format

NUMERACY PRACTICE TEST 4

Instructions

- There are 35 questions.
- You have 45 minutes to complete the test.
- You have to shade one bubble for each multiple-choice question.
- Write your answer in the box for short answer questions.

NAME : ______________________ **SCORE :**__________

NUMERACY YEAR 2

1 How many lines of symmetry does a regular triangle have?

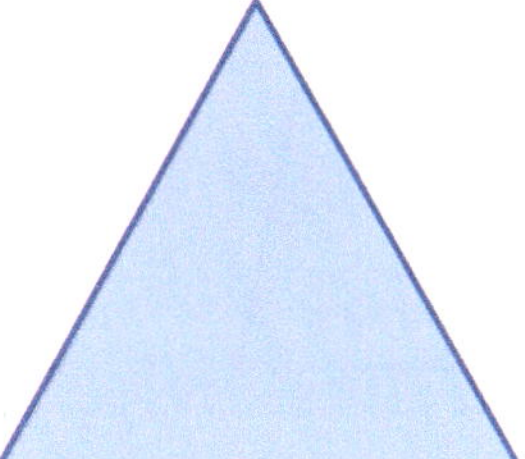

1 ☐ 2 ☐ 3 ☐ 4 ☐

2 What is the smallest number you can make using the following three cards?

You can only use each card once.

3 Adrian, Brian, Charlie and Daniel play a computer game.

The table below shows how long it took each of them to complete a level.

Who was the fastest?

Name	Time
Adrian	59 seconds
Brian	1 minute
Charlie	65 seconds
Daniel	1 minute 4 seconds

4 Which two of the shapes below can be put together to make a square?

A B C D E

A and B ☐ A and D ☐ B and E ☐ C and D ☐

5 Thomas is facing north. He turns clockwise to face south.

How many right angles does he turn through?

6 Steven used a table to record the temperature of some cities in Australia.

The results are shown below.

Sydney	Brisbane	Melbourne	Adelaide	Perth
22°C	27°C	18°C	16°C	21°C

How much warmer was Brisbane than Melbourne?

2°C ☐ 5°C ☐ 7°C ☐ 9°C ☐

7 The bar chart below shows the scores of four students in a Maths competition.

They had to score 10 points or more to get to the next round of the competition.

How many students got to the next round?

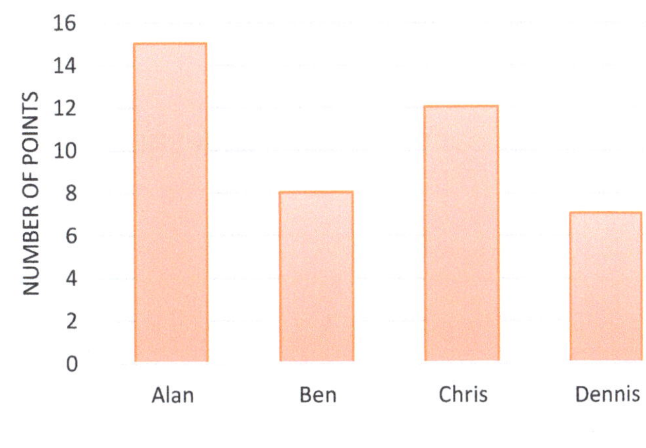

8 Lee's family go to the cinema.

How much does it cost for 2 children and 2 adults?

Movie tickets

Adult $15

Child $10

9 Which of the following calculations has the biggest answer?

- ☐ $70 \div 10$
- ☐ $30 \div 5$
- ☐ $18 \div 2$
- ☐ $48 \div 6$

10 These cars are in line from left to right.

The green car is 3 places away from which car?

red car ☐ blue car ☐ pink car ☐ grey car ☐

11 Three bags of oranges weigh 27 kg.

How heavy is one bag of oranges?

☐

12 The table shows how long 4 students took to complete their school homework.

Name of Student	Time Taken
Liam	1 hour
Noah	45 minutes
Lucas	90 minutes
Elijah	1 hour 20 minutes

Who took the longest time?

Liam ☐ Noah ☐ Lucas ☐ Elijah ☐

13 How many angles are there inside of the figure shown below?

16 ☐ 8 ☐ 6 ☐ 5 ☐

14 Mrs Wilson decided to buy her class of 25 children 8 chocolates each.

How many chocolates did she buy?

☐

15 David is a swimmer. He goes to the pool every day to swim 14 laps. How many laps does he swim in a week?

84 ☐ 98 ☐ 120 ☐ 140 ☐

16 Judy wants to buy 24 pens in total. Judy notices an offer where she can buy 6 pens for $2.
How much does Judy spend if she buys 24 pens with the offer?

6 pens for $2

$6 ☐ $8 ☐ $10 ☐ $12 ☐

17 Pauline played through 10 songs in 1 hour.

How long is each song?

☐ minutes

18 Alex divided his 24 lollies with his 4 good friends.

How many lollies were left over, if Alex and his friends each got the same number of lollies?

1 ☐ 2 ☐ 3 ☐ 4 ☐

19 Which square is the cow in below?

B2 ☐ C2 ☐ B3 ☐ C3 ☐

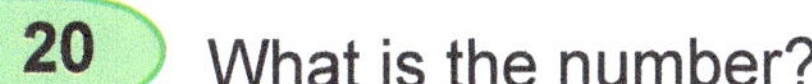

20 What is the number?

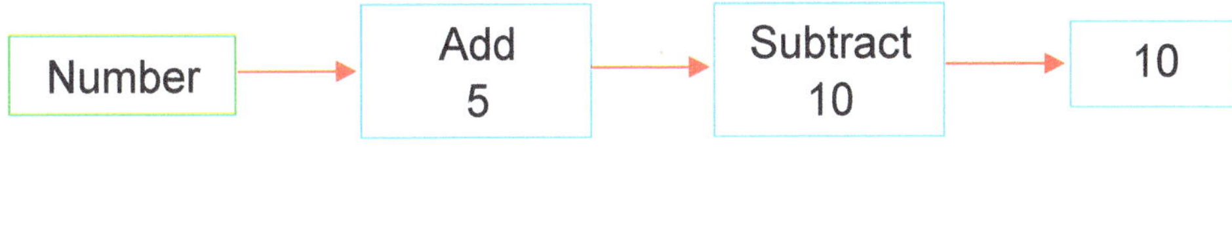

☐

21 There are some chickens on a farm.
If there are a total of 28 legs, how many chickens are there?

14 ☐ 28 ☐ 56 ☐ 112 ☐

22 Choose the correct number that fits the following rule.

500	460	420	380	340	?	260	220	180	140

320 ☐ 300 ☐ 280 ☐ 240 ☐

23 What is the top view of this object?

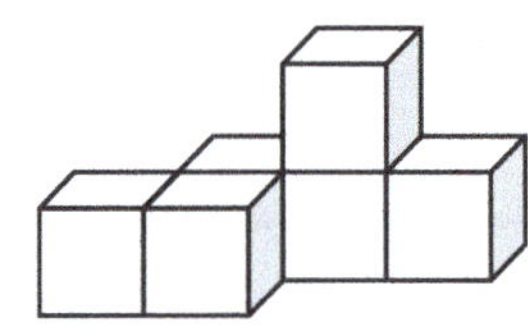

Front

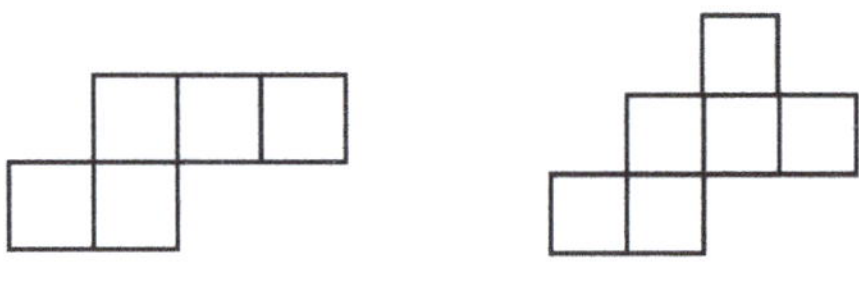

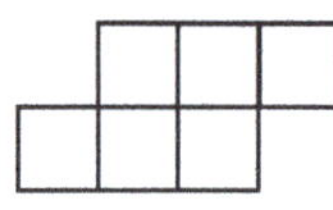

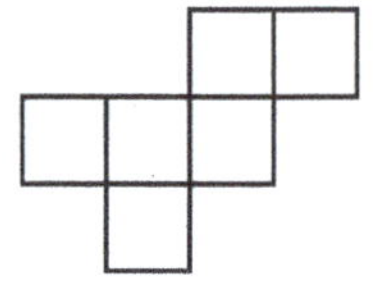

☐ ☐ ☐ ☐

24 Choose the largest angle.

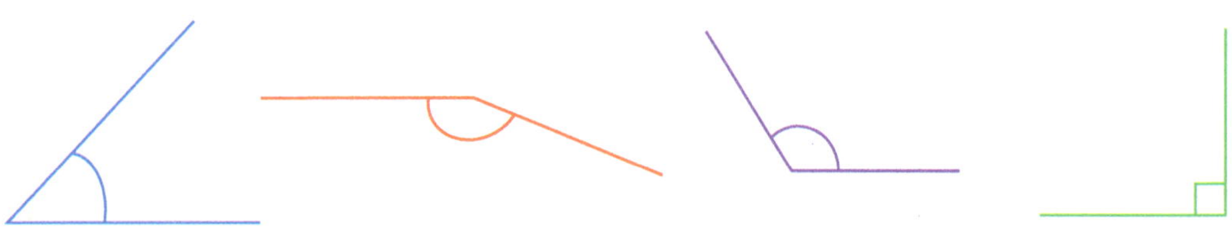

☐ ☐ ☐ ☐

25 What is (8 × 1000) + (3 × 100) + (7 × 10) + (4 × 1) in standard form?

8371 ▭ 8314 ▭ 8374 ▭ 8273 ▭

26 This is a 100 mL measuring container.

How much water is there?

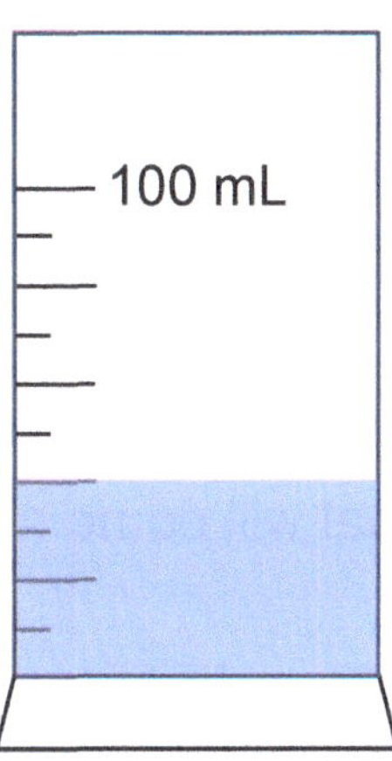

30 mm ▭ 40 L ▭ 30 mL ▭ 40 mL ▭

27 What is the length of the scissors below?

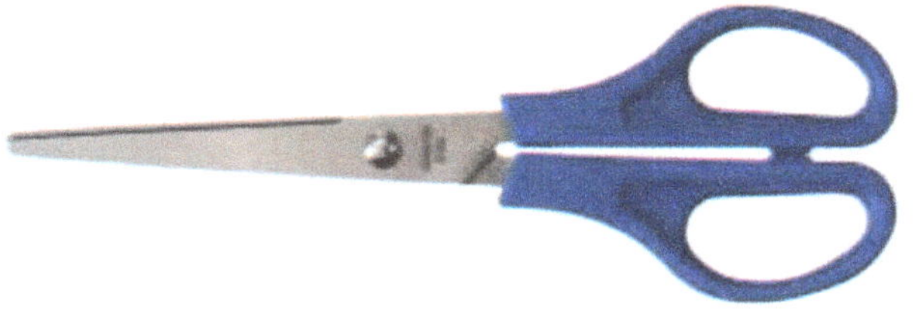

cm 1 2 3 4 5 6 7 8 9 10 11

7 cm ▭ 8 cm ▭ 9 cm ▭ 10 cm ▭

28 What is the perimeter of the following shape?

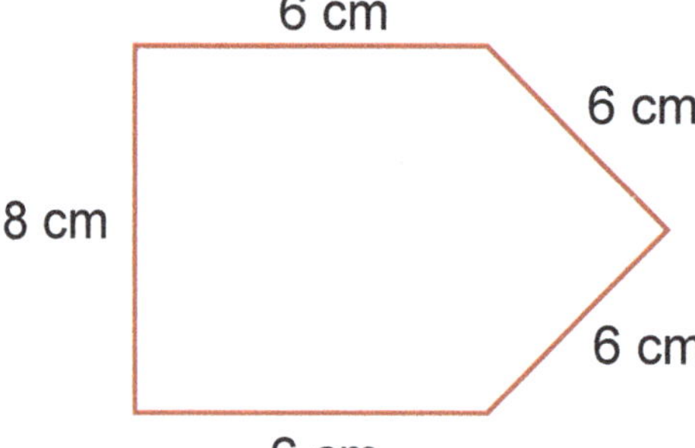

29 What will come next in the pattern below?

30 What is the weight of the watermelon below?

 kg

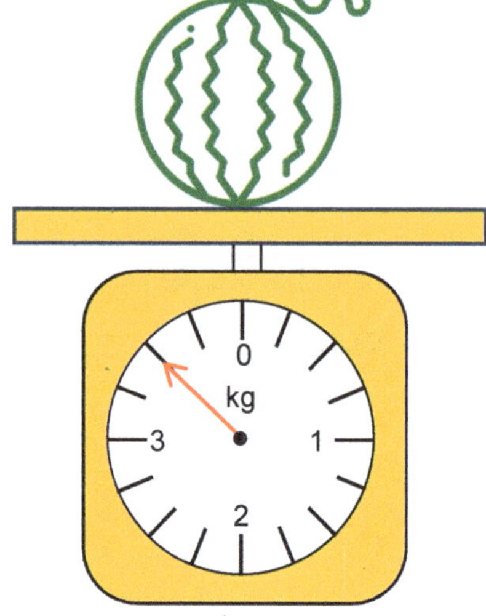

31 Which of these is **not** true?

- [ ] $25 + 3 = 50 - 22$
- [ ] $6 \times 6 = 7 \times 5 + 1$
- [ ] $\frac{1}{2}$ of $18 + 1 = 3 \times 4 - 2$
- [ ] $24 \div 3 = 8 \times 2$

32 Oliver walked 5 minutes to the bus stop and waited 7 minutes for the bus. The bus took 18 minutes to reach his school.

How long did he take to get to school?

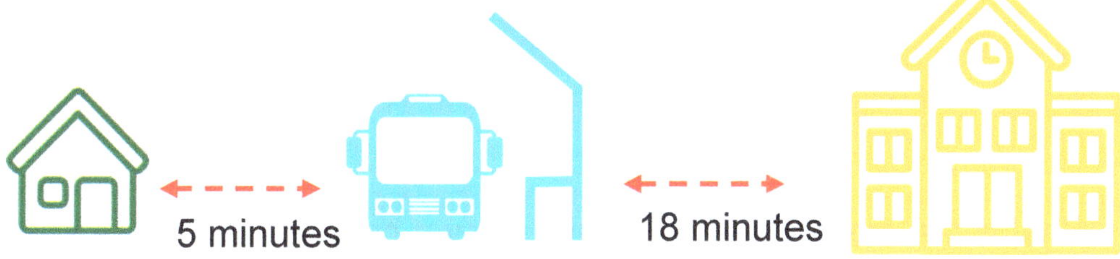

23 minutes	25 minutes	27 minutes	30 minutes
☐	☐	☐	☐

33 In which number below is the value of 3 biggest in?

348, 34, 2030, 853

348 ☐ 34 ☐ 2030 ☐ 853 ☐

34 What is the fraction shown in the shape below?

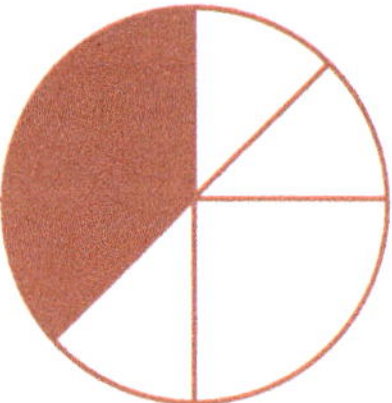

$\frac{2}{6}$ ☐ $\frac{1}{4}$ ☐ $\frac{1}{3}$ ☐ $\frac{3}{8}$ ☐

35 What is the cross-sectional shape shown below?

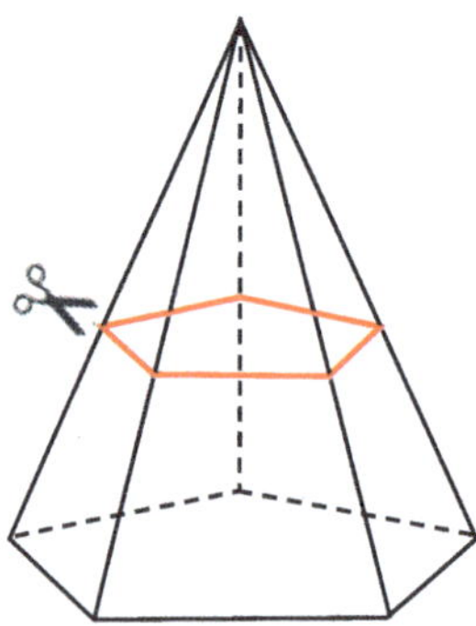

square ☐ rectangle ☐ pentagon ☐ rhombus ☐

Year 2 NAPLAN*-Format

NUMERACY PRACTICE TEST 5

Instructions

- There are 35 questions.
- You have 45 minutes to complete the test.
- You have to shade one bubble for each multiple-choice question.
- Write your answer in the box for short answer questions.

NAME : ______________________ **SCORE :**__________

1 What is (5 × 1000) + (7 × 10) + (4 × 1) equal to?

571 ☐ 547 ☐ 5071 ☐ 5074 ☐

2 Where is 4.5 on the number line?

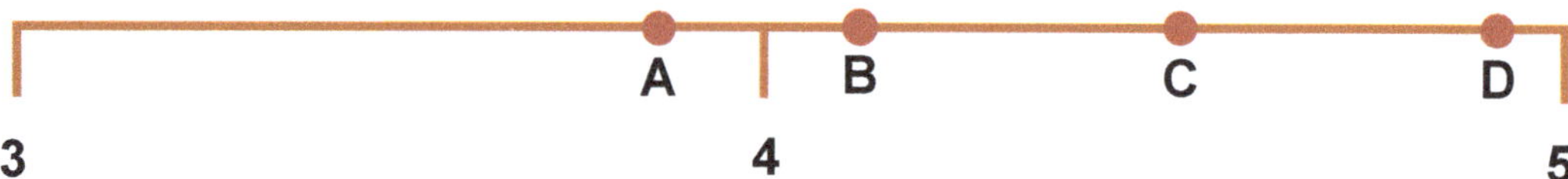

A ☐ B ☐ C ☐ D ☐

3 What 3D shape does the following net form?

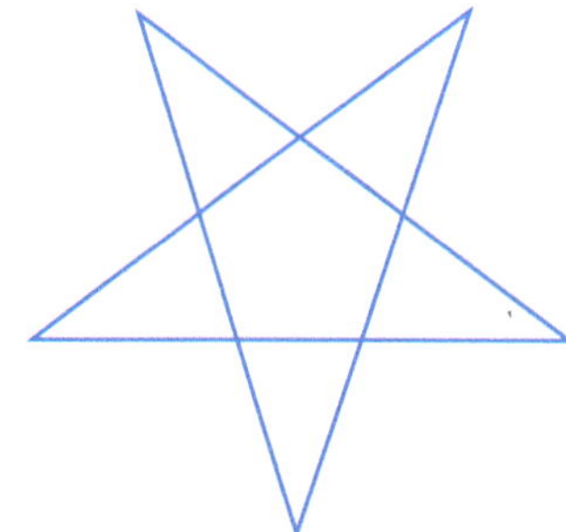

☐ pentagonal pyramid

☐ square pyramid

☐ pentagonal prism

☐ triangular pyramid

4 How would you write 22 as a tally?

- [ ] 
- [ ] 
- [ ] 
- [ ] 

5 Which of the following times is closest to the time displayed on this watch?

9:10	9:14	9:19	9:20
☐	☐	☐	☐

6 What fraction of the triangle is shaded?

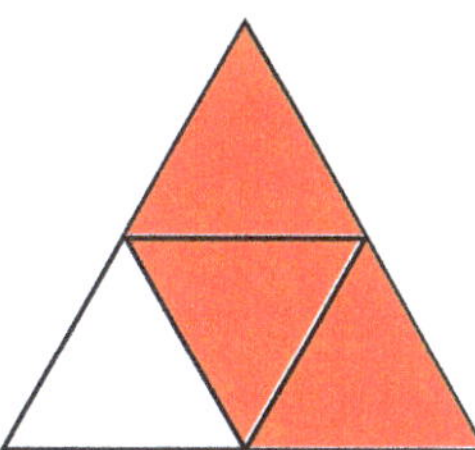

$\frac{1}{2}$	$\frac{2}{3}$	$\frac{3}{4}$	$\frac{3}{5}$
☐	☐	☐	☐

7 Arrange the following numbers in descending order:

2938, 402, 124, 6062

- [ ] 124, 402, 2938, 6062
- [ ] 6062, 2938, 124, 402
- [ ] 6062, 2938, 402, 124
- [ ] 2938, 402, 124, 6062

8 Daniel had 28 stamps. If he added another 35 stamps one day and then another 49 stamps the next, how many stamps does he have in total?

103	108	112	118
☐	☐	☐	☐

9 Ronald spent 2 hours finishing his English and Maths homework. If it took him 1 hour and 20 minutes to finish his English homework, how long did he spend on his Maths homework?

1 hour 20 minutes

☐

10 What is the missing digit below?

$$
\begin{array}{r} 1\square 74 \\ +\ 549 \\ \hline 2023 \end{array}
$$

3 ☐ 4 ☐ 5 ☐ 6 ☐

11 Complete the number pattern.

68, 80, 92, ☐

12 What is the perimeter of the following shape?

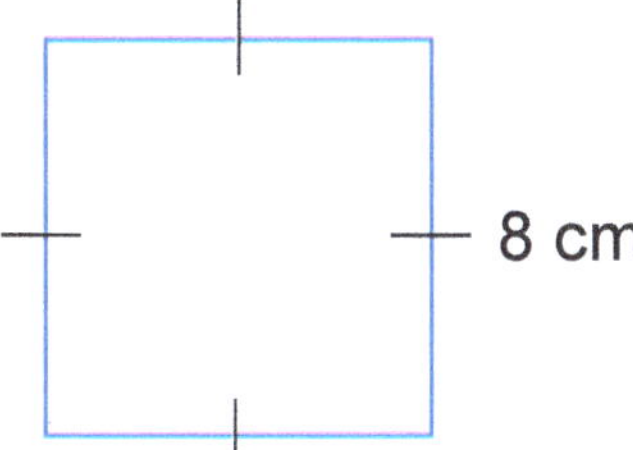

16 cm ☐ 32 cm ☐ 40 cm ☐ 64 cm ☐

13 Jessie received $5 change after giving the cashier $50 to buy 9 exercise books.
How much did each exercise book cost?

$5 ☐ $10 ☐ $15 ☐ $20 ☐

14 If Angela made two necklaces which required 132 and 94 beads, and she had 54 beads left, how many beads did she start off with?

270 ☐ 280 ☐ 290 ☐ 300 ☐

15

Claire's marks (out of 100):	
English	89
Mathematics	99
Science	97

How many more marks did she need to get 300/300?

☐

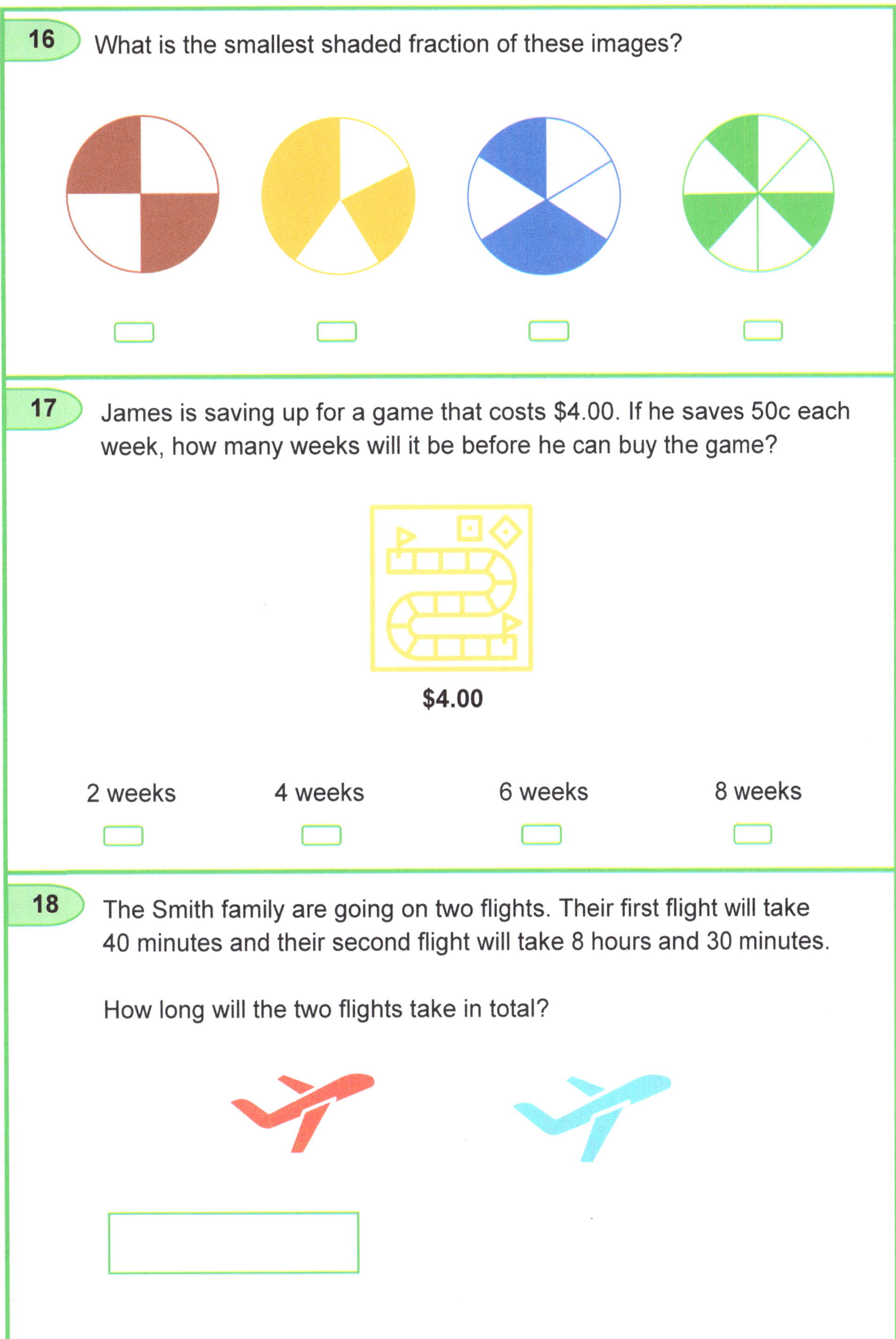

16 What is the smallest shaded fraction of these images?

17 James is saving up for a game that costs $4.00. If he saves 50c each week, how many weeks will it be before he can buy the game?

$4.00

2 weeks 4 weeks 6 weeks 8 weeks

18 The Smith family are going on two flights. Their first flight will take 40 minutes and their second flight will take 8 hours and 30 minutes.

How long will the two flights take in total?

19 Which of the following shapes is **not** symmetrical?

☐ ☐ ☐ ☐

20 Which set of numbers can be put in the empty box in the sorting diagram below?

	Odd	Even
Multiple of 3	3, 9, 15	
Not a multiple of 3	1, 5, 7	2, 4, 8

6 and 10 ☐ 6 and 12 ☐ 6 and 21 ☐ 12 and 21 ☐

21 Diana had 30 candies. She ate 6 candies and shared the rest between her best friends; Emily, Lucy and Elena.

How many candies did each of her friends get?

22 The thermometer on the right shows the temperature in Melbourne.

The temperature is 2°C warmer in Sydney.

What is the temperature in Sydney?

50° 45° 40° 35° 30° 25° 20° 15° 10° 5° 0°

23 What is the total value of the money below?

$6.20 $7.20 $8.20 $9.20

24 Peter rotates the shape below 90° anti-clockwise.

Which of the following shows the rotated shape?

25

33 ÷ 4 = **?** remainder 1

What is the missing number in this calculation?

6 ☐ 7 ☐ 8 ☐ 9 ☐

26 Jason bought a ball and a racket at a sports shop.
The ball cost $2.30 and the racket cost $18.70 more than the ball.
How much did Jason spend altogether?

$2.30

☐

27 What number, when multiplied by 6, gives the same answer as

24 × 2 ?

☐ **× 6 = 24 × 2**

28 Which number is in the **wrong** section of this Venn diagram?

Multiples of 2 | multiples of 3

2, 4, 6 | 12 | 3, 9, 15

6 ☐ 9 ☐ 12 ☐ 15 ☐

29

☐ < 1771

Which of the following numbers could go in the box above?

1870 ☐ 1779 ☐ 1862 ☐ 1769 ☐

30 Which of the following is $\frac{1}{3}$ of a container of water?

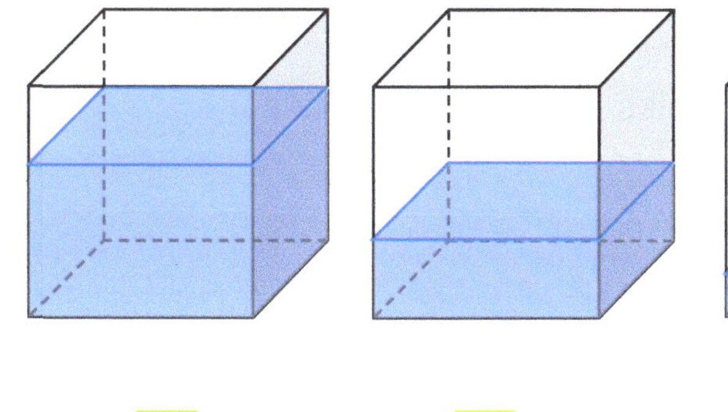

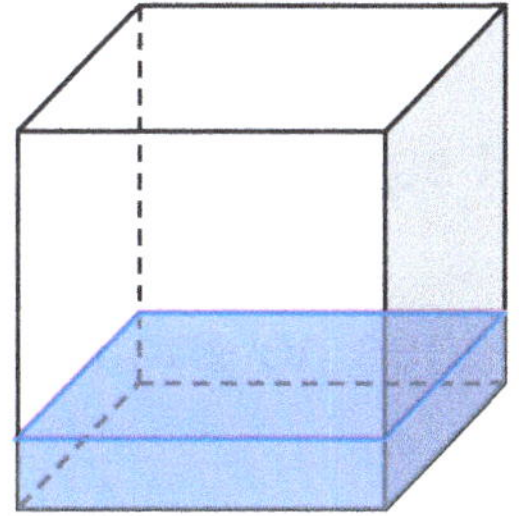

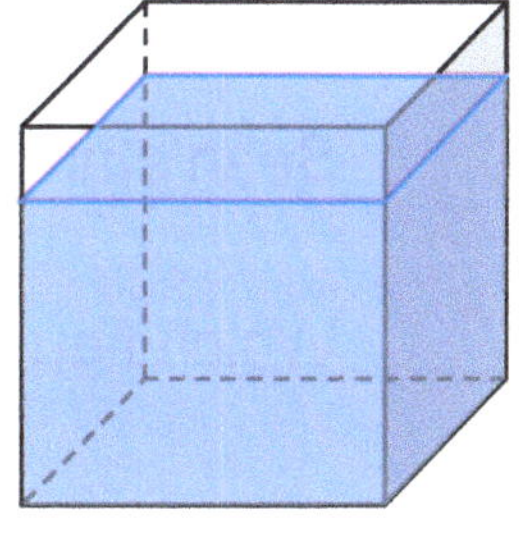

☐ ☐ ☐ ☐

31 A train passes every 15 minutes. How many trains will pass in one hour from now if the next train will come in 5 minutes?

2 trains ☐ 3 trains ☐ 4 trains ☐ 5 trains ☐

32

	A	B	C	D
1				
2				
3				
4				

N

Sean starts at square A2. He walks 2 squares east.

Which figure does he end up with?

☐ ☐ ☐ ☐

33 Form the **smallest** 4-digit number with the digits below.

6 5 2 1

34 Choose the top view of the following shape.

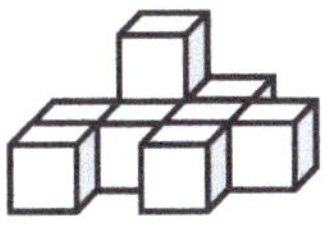

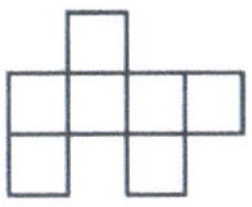

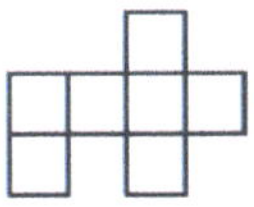

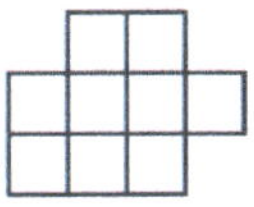

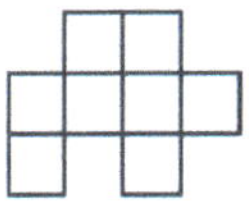

35 What is the number of dots on the side opposite to [3] on the net of a die below?

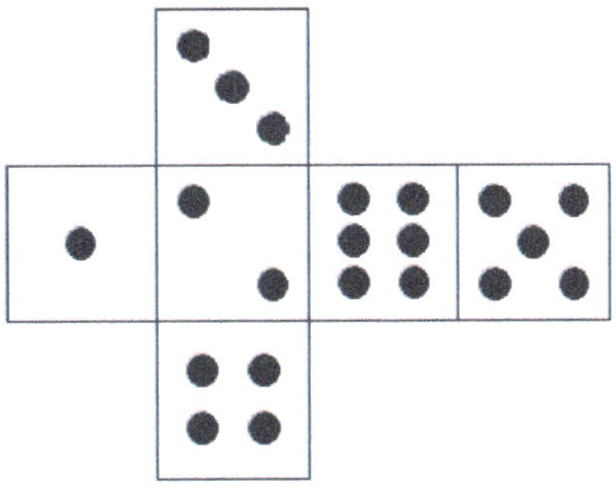

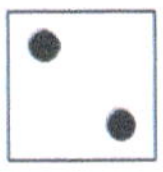

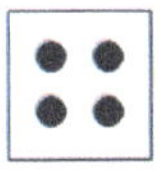

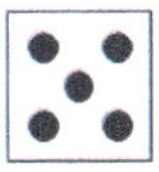

Year 2 NAPLAN*-Format

NUMERACY PRACTICE TEST 6

Instructions

- There are 35 questions.
- You have 45 minutes to complete the test.
- You have to shade one bubble for each multiple-choice question.
- Write your answer in the box for short answer questions.

NAME : ______________________ **SCORE :**__________

NUMERACY YEAR 2

1 A group of children share 12 crayons. Each child gets 3 crayons.

How many children are there in the group?

3 ☐ 4 ☐ 5 ☐ 6 ☐

2 What is the total value of these coins?

$1.70 ☐ $2.00 ☐ $2.30 ☐ $2.80 ☐

3 This year the 7th August is a Tuesday.
What day of the week is 21th August?

Monday ☐ Tuesday ☐ Wednesday ☐ Thursday ☐

4 Simon recorded the number of pets owned by children in his class. The bar chart below shows the results.

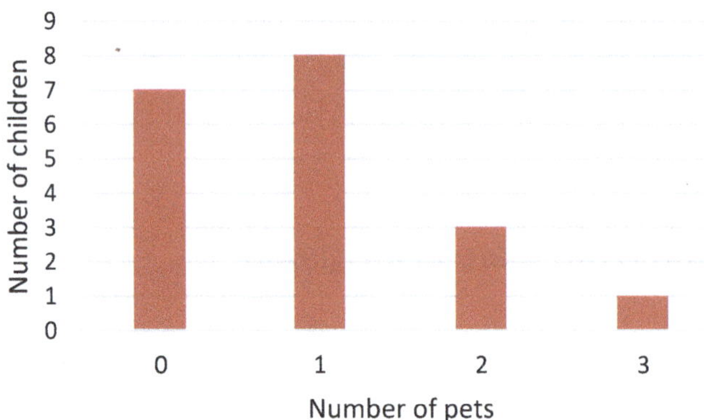

How many children have only 1 pet?

☐

5 There are 24 people on a bus. 7 people get off the bus and 5 people get on.
How many people are on the bus now?

16	20	22	25
☐	☐	☐	☐

6 Vivian buys a book for $9.50 and a birthday card for $1.50.

What change does she get from $20?

$6	$7	$8	$9
☐	☐	☐	☐

7 Thomas completed the graph below to show the size of his friends' shoes.

Daniel
Chris
Benny
Andy

Who had the largest shoes?

Andy ☐ Benny ☐ Chris ☐ Daniel ☐

8 Karen is counting backwards by 5s.

50, 45, ☐ , ? , ☐ , 25, 20

Which number should go in the middle box?

30 ☐ 35 ☐ 40 ☐ 20 ☐

9 Which one of the following solids has the greatest number of faces?

☐ ☐ ☐ ☐

10 An incomplete bus timetable is shown to the right. The time between the arrival of each bus is the same.

When will the next bus come?

Bus Timetable	
1st bus	6:00 am
2nd bus	7:30 am
3rd bus	?

11 What is the next number in this pattern?

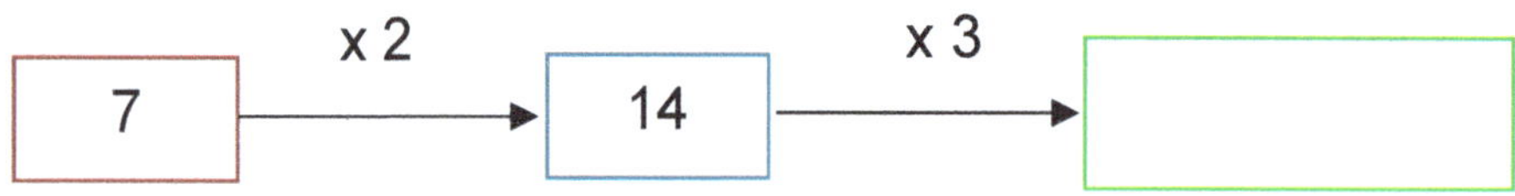

12 Which of the shapes below have the same perimeter?

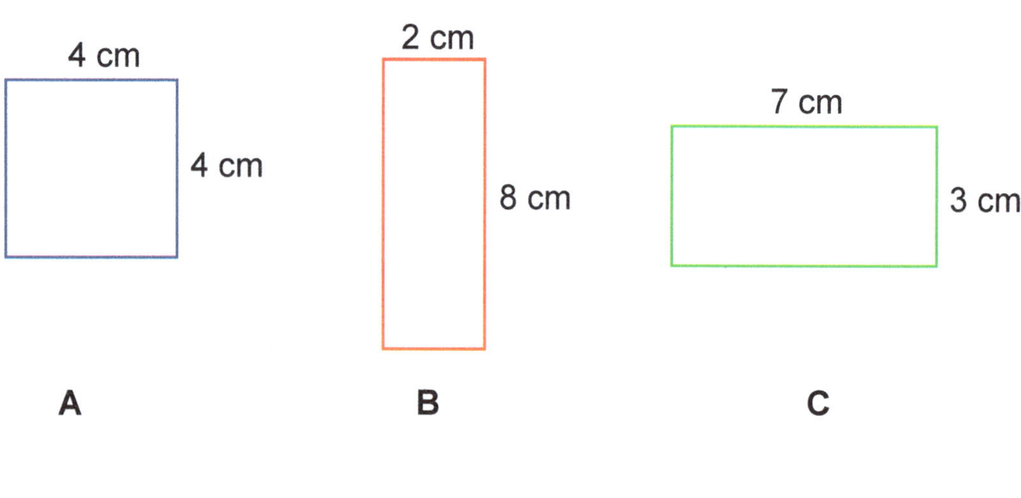

A and B ☐ B and C ☐ A and C ☐ A, B and C ☐

13 Four shapes are made from squares that are all the same size.

Which shape below has one-quarter of the squares shaded?

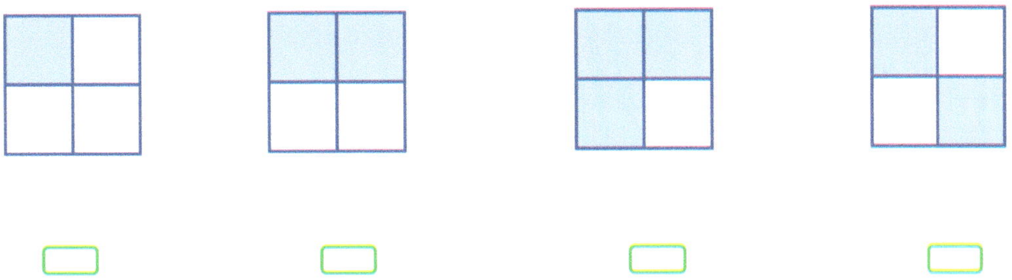

☐ ☐ ☐ ☐

14 What number goes in the empty space?

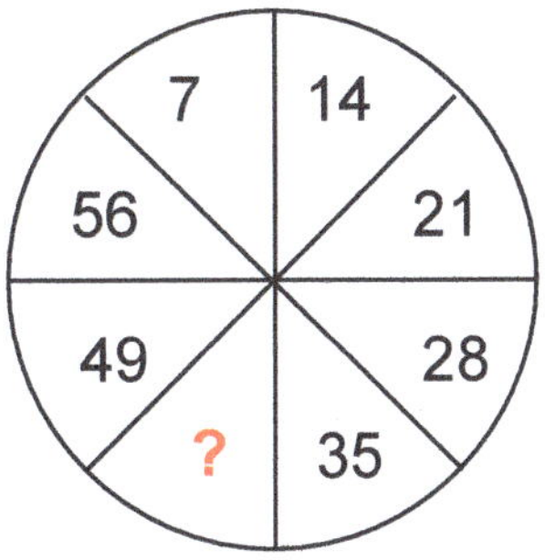

7, 14, 21, 28, 35, ?, 49, 56

15 The graph below shows the favourite colour chosen by students at a school.

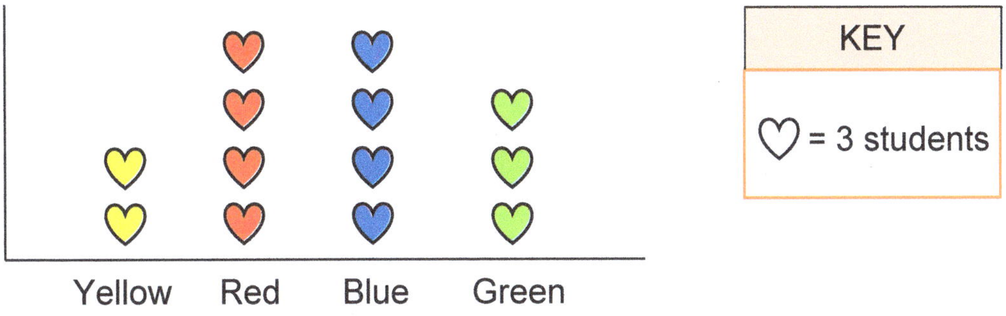

Yellow, Red, Blue, Green

KEY

♡ = 3 students

How many students chose green?

16 Which multiplication is INCORRECT?

- ☐ 14 × 4 = 56
- ☐ 13 × 3 = 39
- ☐ 15 × 5 = 85
- ☐ 48 × 2 = 96

17 What time is the clock below showing?

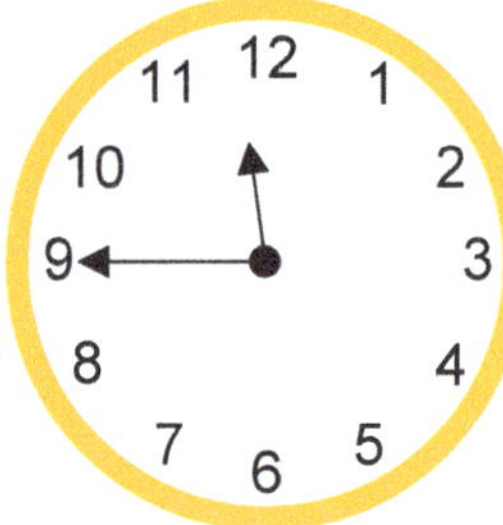

Quarter to 12	Quarter to 11	9 o'clock	12 o'clock
☐	☐	☐	☐

18 How many rectangles can be found in this diagram of a basketball court?

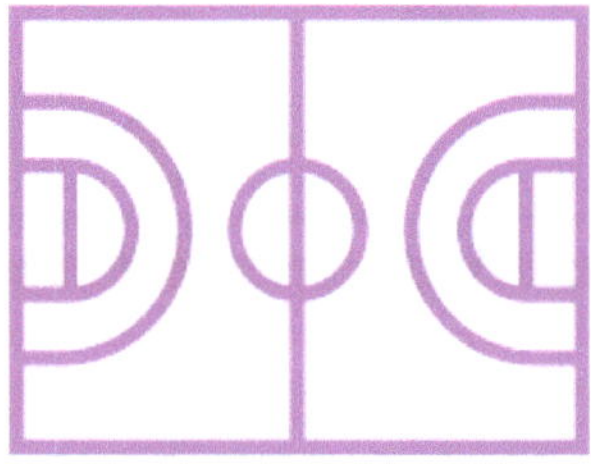

2	3	4	5
☐	☐	☐	☐

19 Look carefully at the numbers in these boxes.

10, 5, 25, 15	4, 32, 20, 16
3, 9, 27, 12	21, 28, 7, ?

Which of the following could be the missing number in the last box?

10 ☐ 19 ☐ 37 ☐ 56 ☐

20

6 ☆ 6 + 6 = 42

Which operation goes where the star is to make the number sentence true?

− ☐ + ☐ × ☐ ÷ ☐

21 What fraction of the hexagon is shaded?

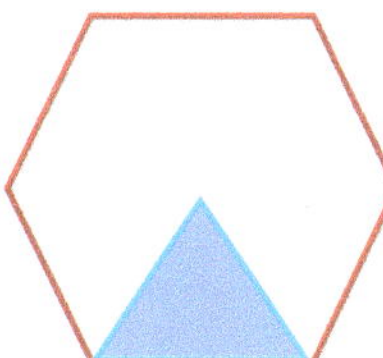

$\frac{1}{3}$ ☐ $\frac{1}{4}$ ☐ $\frac{1}{6}$ ☐ $\frac{1}{8}$ ☐

22 Which solid has one flat surface and one curved surface?

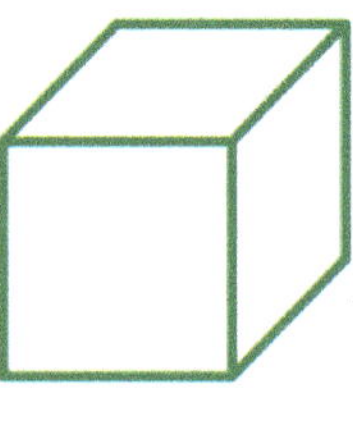

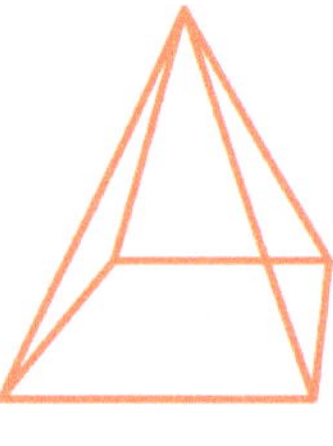

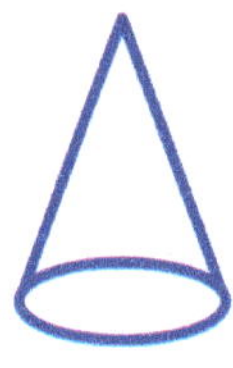

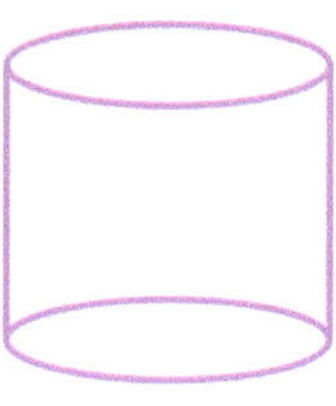

23 Jamie's soccer game started at 9 o'clock. The game went for half an hour.

What time did the game finish?

24 Amelia is 133 cm tall. Luna is 15 cm shorter than Amelia.

How tall is Luna?

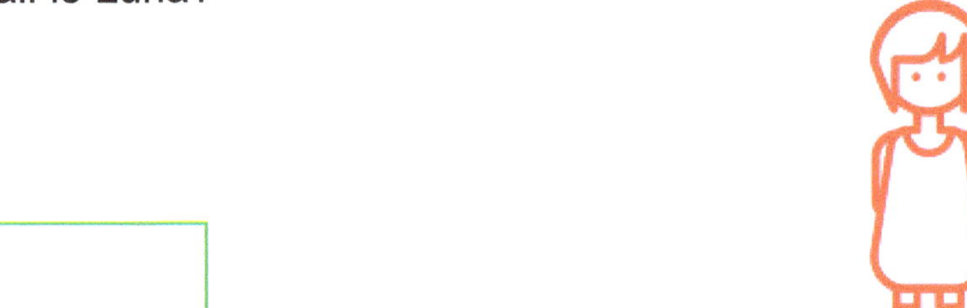

25 Without looking, Sophia took one lolly out of the bag below of 8 lollies.

There is 1 chance in 2 that the lolly was

green ☐ blue ☐ red ☐ pink ☐

26 Richard shares 12 one-dollar coins and 9 twenty-cent coins equally between his 3 grandchildren.

How much money does each grandchild get?

☐

27 Choose the next figure in the sequence below.

?

☐ ☐ ☐ ☐

28 If the following shapes balance each other like so,

How many triangles are needed to complete the balance?

29 Ezra started at 5 and made the following number pattern.

5, 10, 20, 40, 80, ?

What is the next number in the pattern?

30 Belinda is making a calendar. 30th November is a Monday.

December						
		1	2	3	4	5
6	7	8	9	10	11	12
13	14	15	16	17	18	19
20	21	22	23	24	25	26
27	28	29	30	31		

What day is 9th December?

Sunday ☐ Monday ☐ Tuesday ☐ Wednesday ☐

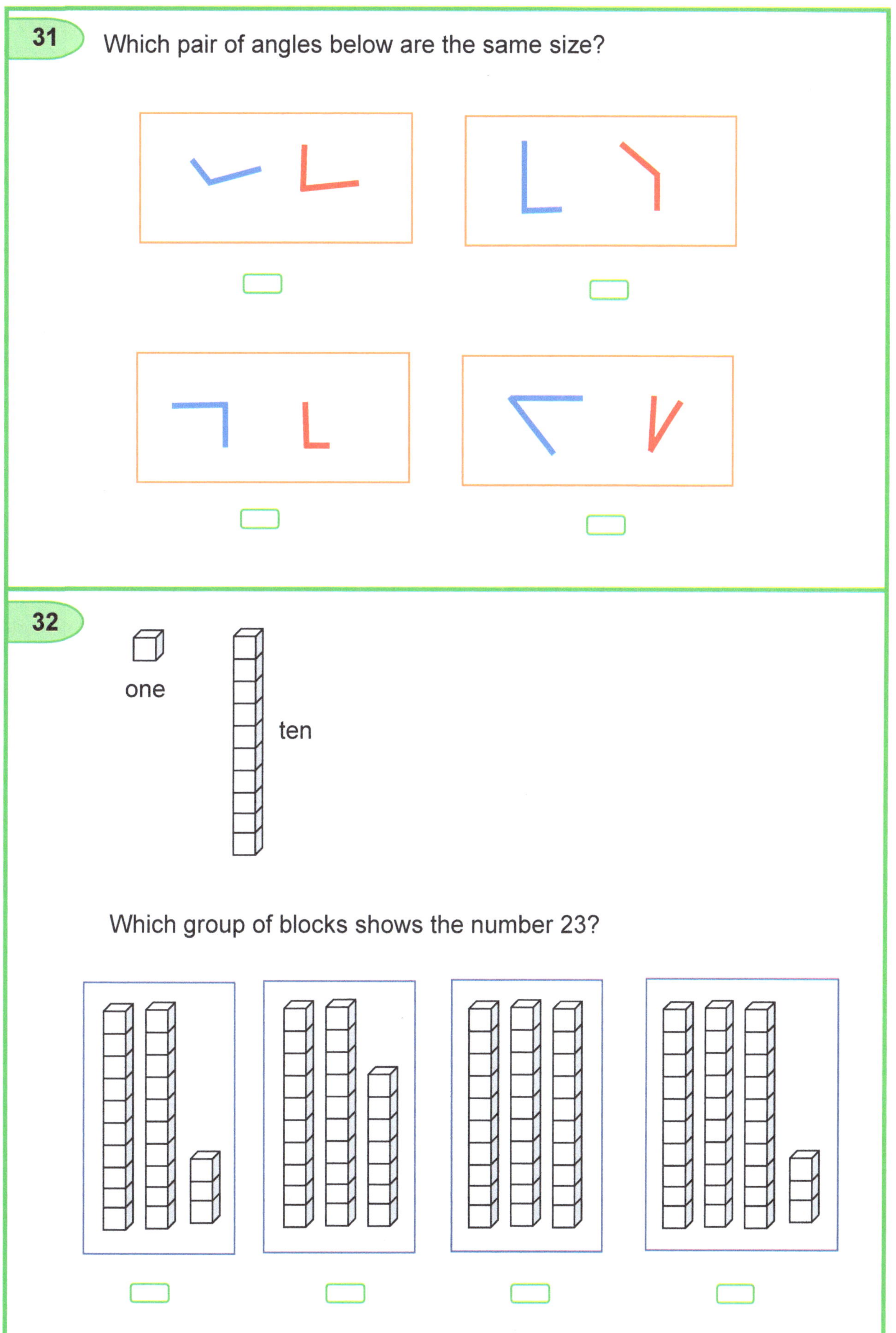
31
Which pair of angles below are the same size?
32
one
ten
Which group of blocks shows the number 23?

33 There are 3 people selling pies at a cricket match.
Each person sells 3 pies a minute.

How many pies are sold in 3 minutes?

6 ☐ 9 ☐ 18 ☐ 27 ☐

34 Choose the shape that will join with the figure without gaps.

 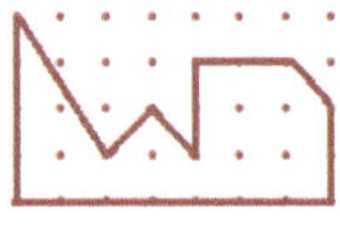  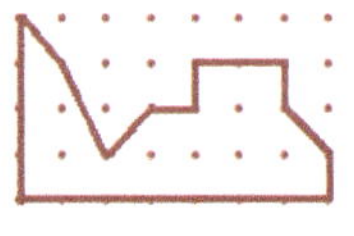

☐   

35 Here is a triangle and a rectangle.

How many of the triangles would you need to make the rectangle?

☐

Year 2 NAPLAN*-Format

NUMERACY PRACTICE TEST 7

Instructions

- There are 35 questions.
- You have 45 minutes to complete the test.
- You have to shade one bubble for each multiple-choice question.
- Write your answer in the box for short answer questions.

NAME : ______________________ **SCORE :__________**

1 There are 120 pages in an exercise book. How many pages are there in 5 such exercise books?

480 ☐ 500 ☐ 570 ☐ 600 ☐

2 I get home from school at 3:30 on Thursdays and I go to soccer lessons which begin twenty minutes later.
What time do my soccer lessons begin?

☐

3 Thomas wants to buy a video game that costs $50.00.

He has saved this money in bank notes.

An extra one of these notes will be needed to make $50.

Which note is that? ☐

4 A teacher gave 4 of her students 5 lollies each.

Which of the following can be used to find how many lollies the teacher gave her students?

- ☐ 4 + 5
- ☐ 4 + 4 + 4 + 4
- ☐ 5 + 5 + 5 + 5
- ☐ 4 + 5 + 4 + 5 + 4 + 5

5 Debbie spent $77.80 at a supermarket. She gave the counter cashier $100. How much change does she receive?

$21.10	$22.20	$23.10	$23.20
☐	☐	☐	☐

6 Gold coins were donated on a mufti day.

If 35 people donated $1 coins and 20 donated $2 coins, how much money was donated in total?

☐

7 Which of the following analog and digital times match?

2:00	6:30	11:55	4:45

8 Jessica makes a three-digit number using the number cards below.

What is the chance that the three-digit number is odd?

1 out of 2 | 1 out of 3 | 1 out of 4 | 1 out of 6

9 Which of the following shapes has 12 edges?

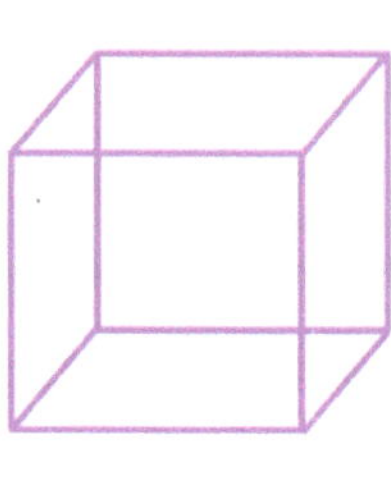
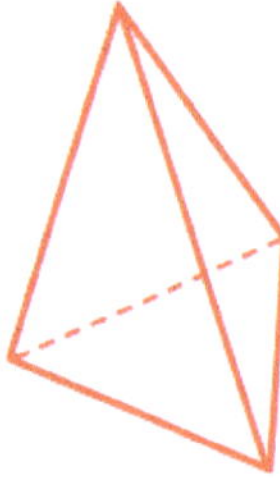
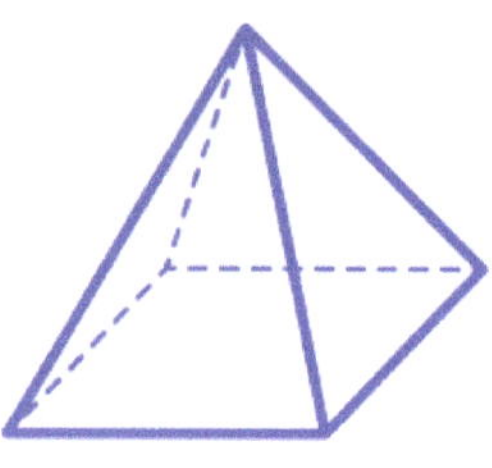

NUMERACY YEAR 2

10 How many degrees is the angle shown below?

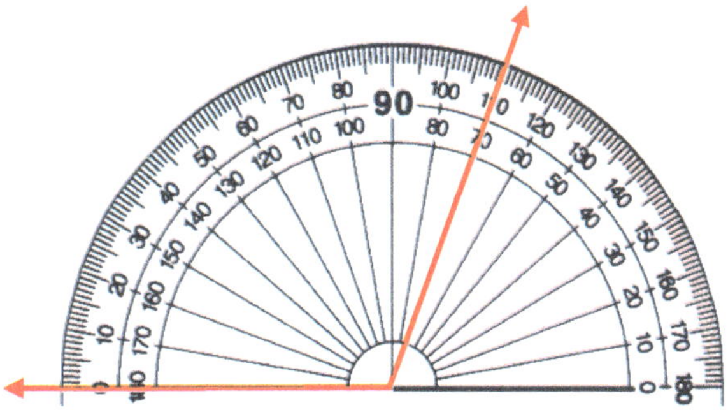

70°	80°	110°	180°
☐	☐	☐	☐

11 Which of the following is the best buy?

$4.00	**$6.00**	**$1.00**	**70c**
☐	☐	☐	☐

12 If the following shapes balance each other like so,

 **and**  **then** 

How many squares are needed to complete the balance?

13 Today is 7th of March 2023.
What is the date 28 days from now?

March						
SUN	MON	TUE	WED	THU	FRI	SAT
		1	2	3	4	5
6	7	8	9	10	11	12
13	14	15	16	17	18	19
20	21	22	23	24	25	26
27	28	29	30	31		

4th of April 2023 ☐ 5th of April 2023 ☐ 6th of April 2023 ☐ 7th of April 2023 ☐

14 Choose the shape that is the correct reflection of the following shape.

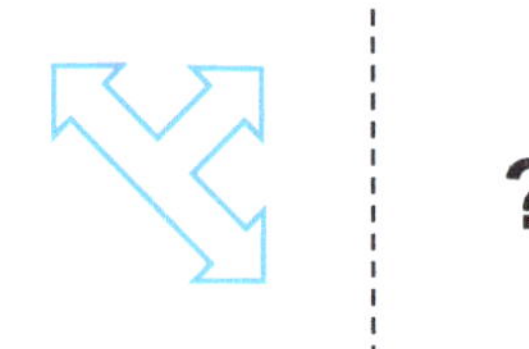

?

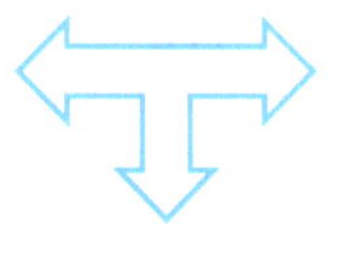

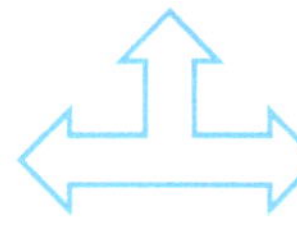

15 What number fills the blank?

4×25 is the same as $10 \times$ ☐

10 ☐ 20 ☐ 30 ☐ 40 ☐

16 Lisa enjoys skipping a lot. She can make 30 jumps every minute.
How many jumps does she make in half an hour?

17

Which number is at ✖ on this number line?

210 ☐ 225 ☐ 250 ☐ 290 ☐

18 Choose the option that is the side view of the given shape.

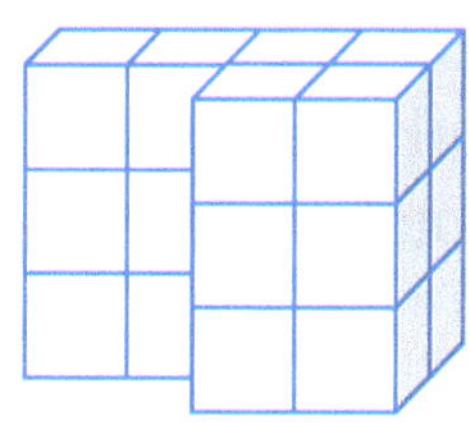

Front

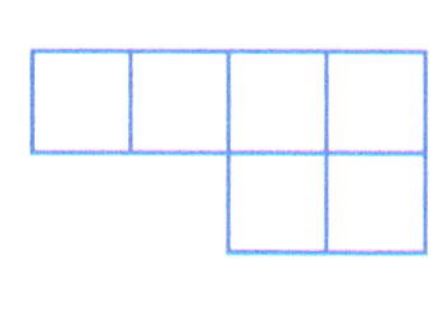

19 Arrange these numbers in ascending order: 2938, 402, 124, 6062

- [ ] 124, 402, 2938, 6062
- [ ] 6062, 2938, 124, 402
- [ ] 6062, 2938, 402, 124
- [ ] 2938, 402, 124, 6062

20 What is the area of the following shaded shape?

12 units^2	14 units^2	22 units^2	24 units^2
☐	☐	☐	☐

21 Rebecca travels 2.3 km by car, 17.7 km by train and 0.8 km by walking in order to get to work.
How far does she travel in total on her way to work?

2.3 km 17.7 km 0.8 km

☐ km

22 Below is a grid.

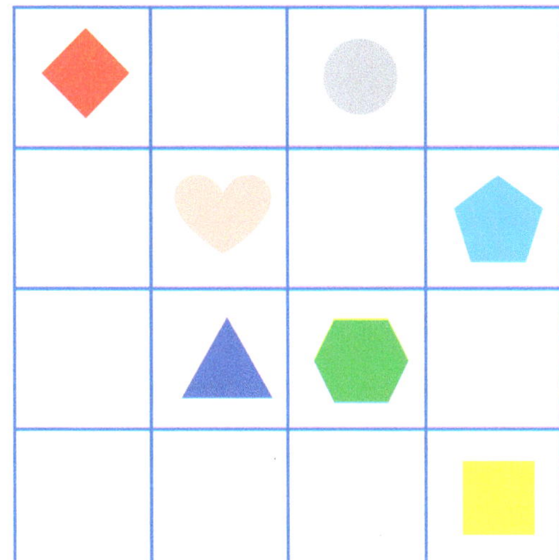

What object is found in the third square from the left, on the second row from the bottom?

triangle ☐ heart ☐ hexagon ☐ pentagon ☐

23 Which of the following ropes is the longest?

☐ 

☐ 

☐ 

☐

24 Jonathan made this number pattern.

3, 6, 9, 12, 15, ...

Which one of these numbers would be in this number pattern?

19	25	35	45
☐	☐	☐	☐

25 A bus has 11 rows of 4 seats. 28 people get on the bus when it is empty and each person sits in a seat.

How many seats are left empty?

26 Lisa is describing a shape. It has four sides, a pair of parallel lines and one line of symmetry.

Which one of these shapes is Lisa describing?

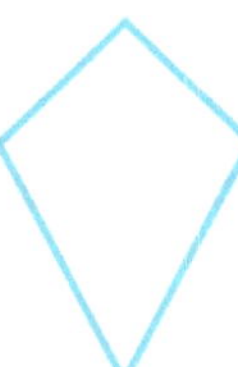  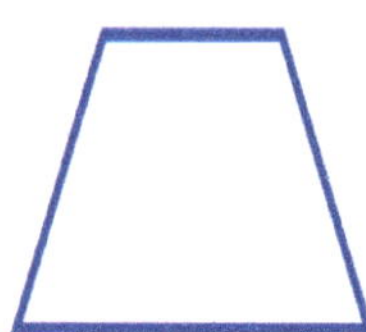 

☐ ☐ ☐ ☐

27

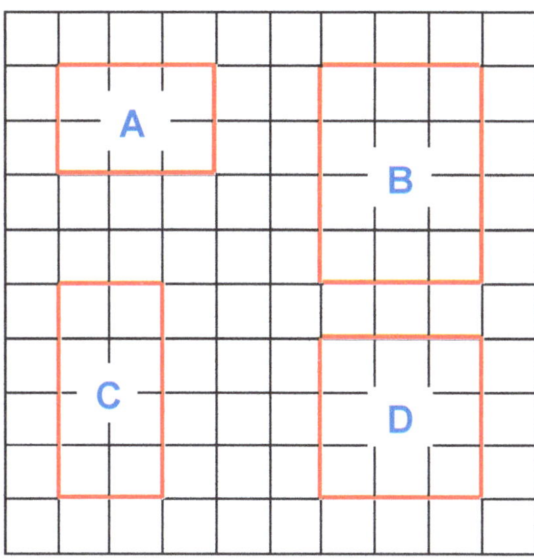

Which two shapes above have the same perimeter?

- [ ] A and B
- [ ] B and C
- [ ] C and D
- [ ] A and C

28 Harry is thinking of a number. It can be divided by both 2 and 3 without any remainder.

Which of the following could be true of Harry's number?

- [ ] It ends in zero.
- [ ] It ends in 3.
- [ ] It ends in 5.
- [ ] It ends in 7.

Questions 29 and 30 are about the timetable below.

Year 2 Tuesday Timetable	
9:00	Handwriting
9:20	Mathematics
10:45	Recess
11:00	English
12:30	Lunch
1:30	Music
2:30	Library
3:00	Home

29 How long is recess?

10 minutes ☐ 15 minutes ☐ 20 minutes ☐ 30 minutes ☐

30 Karen looks at her watch during the English lesson.

Which of these times could her watch show?

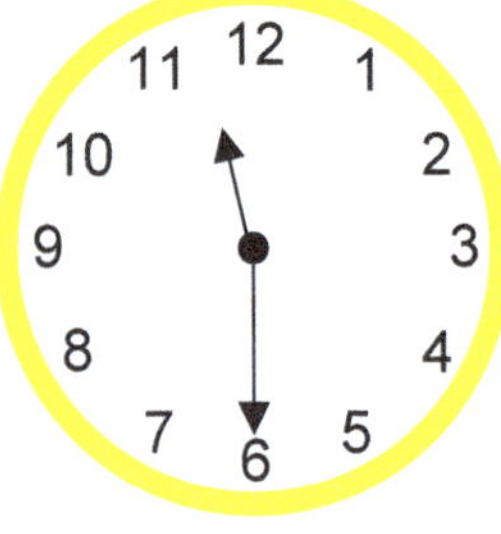

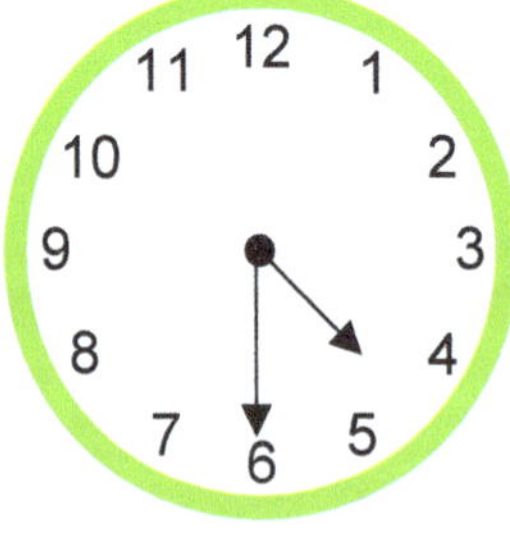

☐ ☐ ☐ ☐

31 A certain company only produces wallets to be between 13 cm and 14 cm long.
Which of these wallets could be made by this company?

14.40 cm	14.60 cm	12.40 cm	13.20 cm
☐	☐	☐	☐

32 Which of the following shapes has the most axes of symmetry?

☐ ☐ ☐ ☐

33 The shapes below are the five faces of a 3D object.

What is the name of the object?

☐

34 A pen costs $2.00 and a book costs $6.30. If I bought 5 pens and 2 books, how much did I have to pay?

$2.00 **$6.30**

35 Which of the following fractions shaded are the same?

A

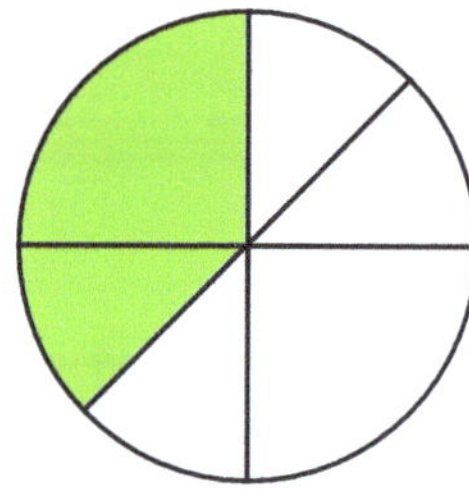

B

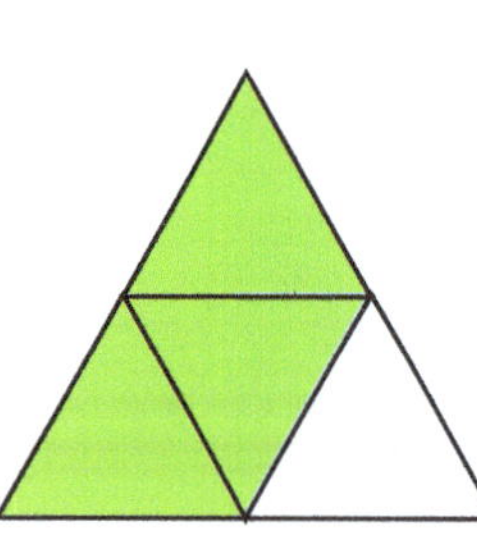

C

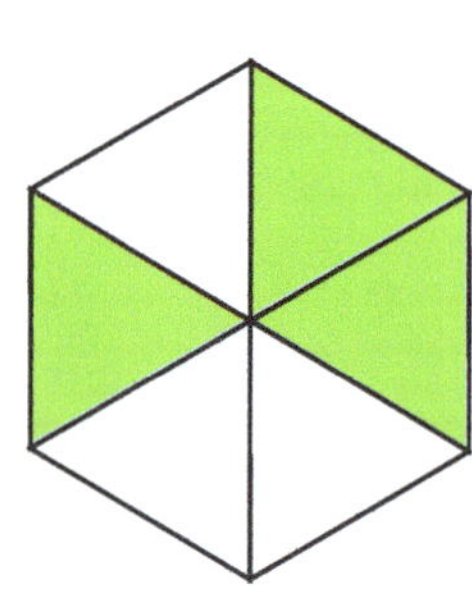

D

and

NUMERACY PRACTICE TEST ANSWERS

NAPLAN Practice Test Answers
NUMERACY 1

Question	Answer	Question	Answer	Question	Answer
1	15	13	2	25	6
2	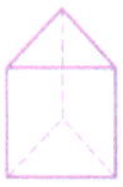	14	54	26	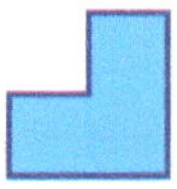
3	8	15	$5	27	36 litres
4	7:30	16	6	28	8
5	210 and 305	17	$11.50	29	23
6	$42	18		30	11:00
7	38	19	145 cm	31	$2.10
8	105	20	5	32	$4.00
9	12	21	6	33	
10	26 kg	22	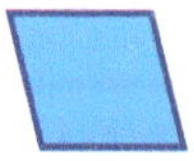	34	32
11	96	23	15	35	6 days
12	12	24			

NAPLAN Practice Test Answers
NUMERACY 2

Question	Answer	Question	Answer	Question	Answer
1	18 cm	13	50	25	29
2	281	14	102	26	
3	$3.00	15		27	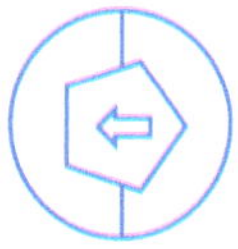
4	80	16	5	28	15
5	49	17	122	29	23
6	85, 105	18	$40	30	8
7	Turn by 90°	19	9	31	7
8	27	20	7	32	south 2 squares, east 3 squares
9	$13.00	21	5	33	432
10	$10.00	22	$11.50	34	5
11	4	23	$\frac{1}{8}$	35	
12	$3.80	24			

NAPLAN Practice Test Answers
NUMERACY 3

Question	Answer	Question	Answer	Question	Answer
1	544	13	26	25	5 kg
2	15	14	250 cm	26	4
3	3	15	10	27	72
4	$230	16		28	
5	$240	17	2:45	29	14
6	16	18	$\frac{3}{8}$	30	Thursday
7	48	19	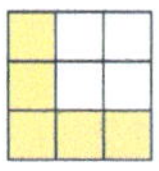	31	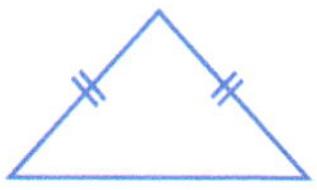
8	66	20	A hexagon has 6 sides.	32	8
9	27	21	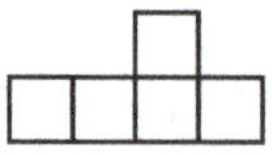	33	09:00
10	10	22	9742	34	$25
11	25	23	4	35	
12	$1.50	24	cone		

NUMERACY YEAR 2

NAPLAN Practice Test Answers
NUMERACY 4

Question	Answer	Question	Answer	Question	Answer
1	3	13	8	25	8374
2	189	14	200	26	40 mL
3	Adrian	15	98	27	7 cm
4	B and E	16	$8	28	32 cm
5	2	17	6	29	
6	9°C	18	4	30	3.5
7	2	19	C2	31	$24 \div 3 = 8 \times 2$
8	$50	20	15	32	30 minutes
9	$18 \div 2$	21	14	33	348
10	Blue car	22	300	34	$\frac{3}{8}$
11	9 kg	23	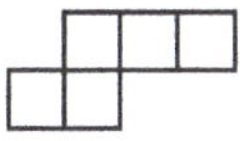	35	pentagon
12	Lucas	24			

NAPLAN Practice Test Answers
NUMERACY 5

Question	Answer	Question	Answer	Question	Answer
1	5074	13	$5	25	8
2	C	14	280	26	$23.30
3	pentagonal pyramid	15	15	27	8
4		16	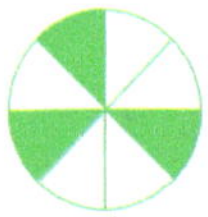	28	6
5	9:14	17	8 weeks	29	1769
6	$\frac{3}{4}$	18	9 hours 10 minutes	30	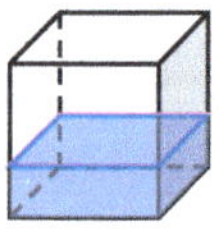
7	6062, 2938, 402, 124	19		31	4 trains
8	112	20	6 and 12	32	
9	40 minutes	21	8	33	1256
10	4	22	27°	34	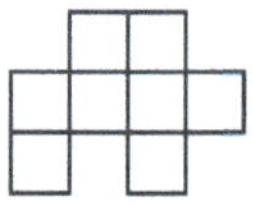
11	104	23	$8.20	35	
12	32 cm	24			

NUMERACY YEAR 2

NAPLAN Practice Test Answers
NUMERACY 6

Question	Answer	Question	Answer	Question	Answer
1	4	13	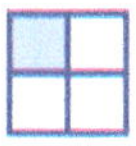	25	Blue
2	$2.00	14	42	26	$4.60
3	Tuesday	15	9	27	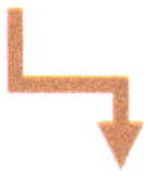
4	8	16	15 × 5 = 85	28	1
5	22	17	quarter to 12	29	160
6	$9	18	5	30	Wednesday
7	Benny	19	56	31	
8	35	20	×	32	
9	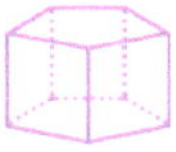	21	$\frac{1}{6}$	33	27
10	9:00 am	22		34	
11	42	23		35	6
12	B and C	24	118 cm		

NAPLAN Practice Test Answers
NUMERACY 7

Question	Answer	Question	Answer	Question	Answer
1	600	13	4th of April 2023	25	16
2	3:50	14		26	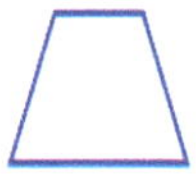
3	$10	15	10	27	C and D
4	5 + 5 + 5 + 5	16	900	28	It ends in zero.
5	$22.20	17	250	29	15 minutes
6	$75	18	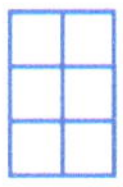	30	
7	4:45	19	124, 402, 2938, 6062	31	13.20 cm
8	1 out of 3	20	14 units^2	32	
9	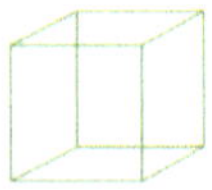	21	20.8 km	33	Square pyramid
10	110°	22	Hexagon	34	$22.60
11	 $1.00	23		35	A and B
12	4	24	45		